Three Stories Leaders Tell

The WHAT and WAY of Using Stories to Lead

Christine Cavanaugh-Simmons

Three Stories Leader Tell: The What and Way of Using Stories to Lead
By Christine Cavanaugh Simmons
1. Leadership 2. Change Management 3. Culture Change 4. Strategic Planning
ISBN: 978-1-4675-2599-2

Cover design by David Lutz

Printed in the United States of America

Authority Publishing
11230 Gold Express Dr. #310-413
Gold River, CA 95670
800-877-1097
www.AuthorityPublishing.com

Table of Contents

worlds

words

pathway

houseOfbeing

Narratives

Stories

Overview

"All change is linguistic."

– Peter Block

Introduction

In today's fast-moving organizations, helping people make sense of the forces that determine the success of their efforts is a key responsibility of leadership. And the spoken or written narratives that a leader develops and shares about his or her organization represent a primary vehicle for inspiring their organization to reach meaningful goals.

At the heart of all leadership narratives is the story-telling process. The stories that we tell about who we are, what our company is, and where we're heading, inform our shared view of who we are and what is possible. A true leader both shapes and blends all the voices of the organization into a message that everyone can internalize and successfully act upon.

Leaders must continually strive to bridge the gap between what is and what will or could be in their organization's culture. Using stories to their fullest potential is one of the most potent tools available for bridging that gap – and that bridge is created by the leader's expression of carefully-crafted words, metaphors, and stories. Let me share an example:

Jan Carlzon took over Scandinavian Airlines when it was 14th of the 17 airlines in Europe, and close to bankruptcy. He believed that his primary job as CEO was to communicate a message to his employees that he strongly believed in – that each person's work mattered. Here's a story he told hundreds of times to create the drumbeat guiding every member of his organization every day in all that they did:

"Last year each of our ten million customers came in contact with approximately five SAS employees, and this contact lasted an average of 15 seconds each time. This means that SAS is 'created' 50 million times a year, 15 seconds at a time. These 50 million 'moments of truth' are the moments that ultimately determine whether SAS will succeed or fail as a company. They are the moments when we must prove to our customers that SAS is their best alternative."

This simple phrase, "moment of truth," was translated into actions, management practices, and a flattened organization which all helped turn SAS around. These influential words also inspired a wave of customer service initiatives at British

Airlines, Japan Airlines and other hospitality organizations around the world. Carlzon demonstrated how the power of a leader's words can bridge the gap between what is and what can be, connecting an entire organization to a shared purpose and identity.

This guide will help you develop your ability to tell the three types of stories that are most commonly used to lead organizations. In order to more fully unleash your power to lead through the narrative process, the following capabilities will be built:

- Reflective appreciation for the people and events that have influenced you
- Clarity regarding your current intentions, beliefs and values
- The ability to tell stories that engage and reflect meaning to your audience
- Techniques for personally connecting with your message
- The capacity to deliver your story with memorable impact
- Confidence that your narrative is interpreted and translated into effective action

Each section of the guidebook will provide specific steps needed to develop a narrative – **the "what"** – and then how to work with and within your organization to ensure that your story delivers the desired impact – **the "way."**

Definitions of Story, Storytelling, and Narrative Process

There is a lot of debate about the definition of these words, and many scholars of far more heft than I have written thoughtfully and provocatively about these definitions. Keeping the guide's purpose of helping leaders drive change with narratives in mind, I have arrived at the definitions on page 6. I followed the guidance of two teachers, Manfred Jahn and Ismail Talib.

As Ismail Talib states in his e-book, *Narrative Theory: A Brief Introduction*, "One problem we may face in the definition of narrative is that we all seem to know what stories and narrative are, so one wonders whether one should define it at all."

My belief is that if these words don't mean something specific then they don't mean anything which causes confusion and disconnects.

The confusion that I have seen reminds me of the parable of the eight blind men and the elephant. We all have our own experience of storytelling but rarely have stepped back to understand the whole elephant and how each part – the tail, the trunk, the leg – all inform something much larger than the "tree trunk," "rope," or "fan" the blind men incorrectly identified through only one element of the elephant.

It's my hope to leave each user of this guide with a much more informed and complete understanding of the power of stories, storytelling, and the narrative process which starts with the following definitions.

"Blind monks examining an elephant" by Itcho Hanabusa.

en.wikipedia.org/wiki/Blind_men_and_an_elephant

What

Story: a message which captures a specific event or moment the story teller has personally experienced or created. The story can come in the form of an anecdote, a parable, or myth.

Way

Storytelling: how the narrative is told which includes arrangement, emphasis, de-emphasis; use of voice, body, media platforms, and timing.

What and Way

Narrative Process: content **and** the process of interpretation; the content has a plot line, metaphors, events, actions, with a complete "reality" including a coherent set of beliefs and assumptions. A dynamic, internal and external, human process of discourse and meaning making which is not separate from the story and storytelling.

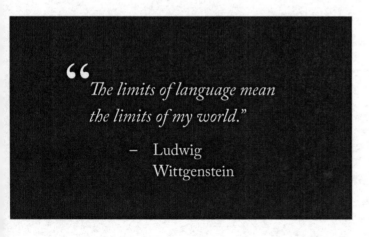

" *The limits of language mean the limits of my world.*"

– Ludwig Wittgenstein

The Three Narratives

This guide will help a leader reflect, construct, deliver, and assess the impact of the three leadership narratives. The three narratives are as follows:

Who am I?

This narrative provides context and the "Why?" an individual is called to lead. It conveys the underlying beliefs and assumptions that guide the leader's actions and decisions. Leaders new to the organization, new to a role, or during times of major change will need to share personal stories that are relevant to the circumstances. Most people want to know what the motives of the leader are when they are unknown quantities or when that leader is asking something of them.

Who are we?

This narrative is called many different things; Genesis Story, Springboard Story, or the Shared Identity Story. A group identity story will remind, renew, and inspire people about what they have accomplished in the past, what they stand for, and in some cases how they have faced adversity and persevered. The organizations shared narrative defines identity and a shared purpose. "Who are we becoming?" is another version of this narrative that pulls people into a future identity that the group's larger narrative points toward as an aspiration.

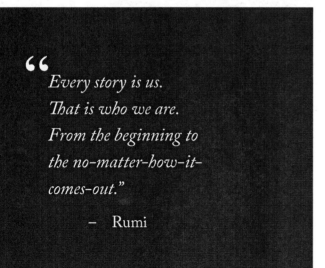

> " *Every story is us.*
> *That is who we are.*
> *From the beginning to*
> *the no-matter-how-it-*
> *comes-out."*
>
> – Rumi

Where are we going?

"Strategic Narrative" will be used to describe this narrative going forward. In the simplest terms, a Strategic Narrative defines the choices the group must make and the "better place" these choices will take the group once they are acted upon. It can also include stories which reflect the author's motives, teaching anecdotes, and stories that build a collective identity. A well-crafted Strategic Narrative has a strategic blueprint, with clear guidance on **how** to move toward the desired goal or vision.

More importantly, the Strategic Narrative is not just a "what" but a "way" to engage others in the ongoing conversations that guide change. Typically this requires iterative cycles of conversation across the organization before and after a Strategic Narrative is decided upon, and then broadly communicated.

Steps to Follow

This guide will take a leader through the following steps for each of the three narratives:

Reflection

How to do the self reflection which helps you select the events in a time-bound, logical plot line for an effective narrative.

Construction

How to craft the narrative, using the ideal narrative structure, words, metaphors, stories, and themes.

Examples of the three narratives that are available in the public domain are somewhat limited due to the content of these narratives. The author has sought to use narratives that illustrated the desired elements over the most currently relevant content.

Delivery & Impact

How to put the methods or processes in place to deliver the narratives and to ensure that the interpretive process is participative and has the intended impact.

Note: If you are new to the use of narratives to lead, some of the steps suggested could be enhanced with the support of an experienced professional. Throughout the guide you will see the "Go Deeper" segments. See our resource page on the website for additional tools and techniques.

Go Deeper

Suggestions for more in-depth work or additional methods available to a leader will appear in these sections throughout the guide.

thinkOtherwise

Inspiration
courageous
Leadership
embodied
takeElsewhere authentic
words THAT heal

Writing the "Who am I?" Narrative

"Knowing others is intelligence; knowing yourself is true wisdom. Mastering others is strength; mastering yourself is true power."

– Norman Schwarzkopf

Introduction – "Who am I?"

When people choose to follow someone, they do so because they understand who that leader is, what they stand for, what is behind the decisions they make, and why they are asking followers to take their lead. The most scalable method for letting people know who the leader is is the use of the "Who am I?" story. This type of narrative uses the leader's life experiences to reveal their beliefs, values, and philosophy. There are four important considerations a leader might have to resolve before sharing revealing personal stories.

The first consideration is that the leader **doesn't see vulnerability as appropriate or may even believe it to be undermining of leadership.** If vulnerability is accepted as a way to demonstrate personal strength, this means the leader is "comfortable being found by the world," according to the poet David Whyte. This means a comfort with being seen by others – complete yet flawed.

The second consideration is that it's **not worth the time to reflect on the events, people, and personal choices they've made that guide their current beliefs, choices, and actions.** The events of the leader's life must be examined and made more accessible so that the "who am I" narrative which is running in the background like an operating system is anchored in key events that can be shared with others.

Another consideration could be that **sharing personal stories has nothing to do with what they want to make happen in the organization.** Telling personal stories ensures that the leader is authoring the narrative which explains the why and what of their actions vs. leaving others to interpret and then formulate their own narrative. In the absence of the leader's narrative, as the group observes and interact with the leader they will build their own narrative about that leader. Often, introverted leaders shrink from talking about themselves and some even find it counter to cultural messages they received growing up. This is a real barrier to overcome. But it must

> " *Few things are more dangerous than a leader with an unexamined life.*"
>
> – John C. Maxwell

be – because if the leader doesn't author their own narrative they will likely lose control of that narrative – and quickly.

The final consideration is that **personal narrative just does NOT belong in the organizational domain**. On the contrary, leadership **is** personal. It's not a performance or a polished product to be placed on display. People follow leaders because they believe they know who they are, they trust their perception because the leader's words match actions and are consistent over time. This is at the heart of trust.

Working with narrative begins with understanding how your personal stories have shaped you. This will require examining beliefs you want to be free of and choosing those which support a meaningful definition of who you are as a leader. Where in your personal narrative about leadership might you be stuck in taken-for-granted beliefs?

Reflection – "Who am I?"

Events That Support Your "Who am I?" Story

My Leadership Plot Line

The value of completing a Leadership Plot Line is to:

- recall significant – peak or painful – experiences

- build a comprehensive list of influences

- catalogue experiences, events, and role models that shaped who you are as a leader

Review the sample personal Leadership Plot Line on the next page.

Sample:

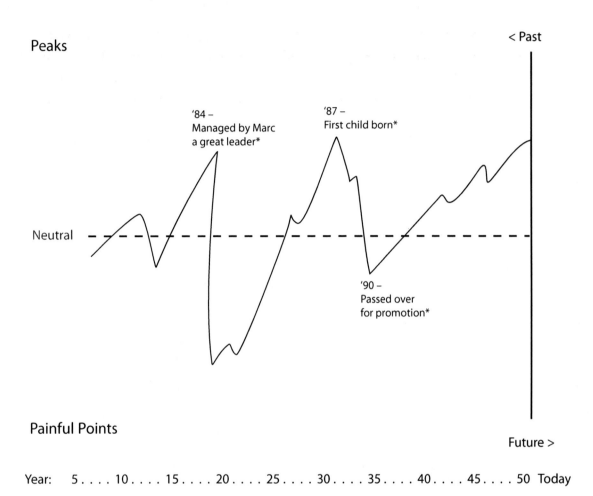

Peaks

'84 –
Managed by Marc
a great leader*

'87 –
First child born*

< Past

Neutral

'90 –
Passed over
for promotion*

Painful Points

Future >

Year: 5 . . . . 10 . . . . 15 . . . . 20 . . . . 25 . . . . 30 . . . . 35 . . . . 40 . . . . 45 . . . . 50 Today

* The points along the time line can be linked to work experiences or significant personal events that shaped you as a leader.

Worksheet

My Leadership Plot Line Inventory

Step One: On the Brainstorm worksheet, write out all of the significant experiences and circumstances surrounding influential people you have had in your personal or work life. Don't sort for painful or peak; just get them down on paper. Finish with rating and anchoring the events in time as you see in the example on page 17.

BRAINSTORM		
EXPERIENCE Event, Key person	**RATING** Peak or Painful	**YEAR**
Example: Marco our first child is born, becoming a First Time Father and experiencing a love that I didn't know was possible.	Peak	1987

17

BRAINSTORM		
EXPERIENCE Event, Key person	**RATING** Peak or Painful	**YEAR**

Sort & Label Your Leadership Plot Line

Step Two: Out of all of these items on pages 17-18, which seem to be most relevant to who you are as a leader? Who were most influential and what experience(s) did you share with these people?

Place the events as points above and below the neutral line that correspond to the time line, labeling them with a short descriptor and the date. Your last step is to connect them into one line.

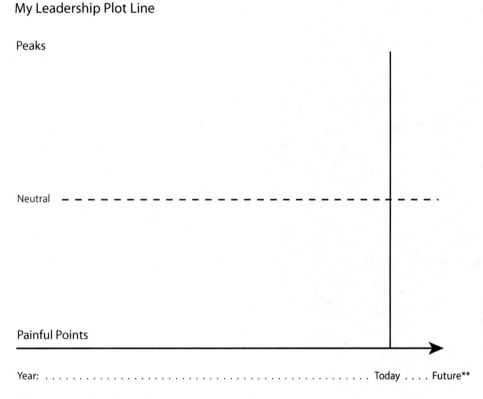

My Leadership Plot Line

Peaks

Neutral

Painful Points

Year: . . . . Today . . . . Future**

** How you think anticipated future events might influence you may or may not be something
you include in your narrative. See page 21 for reflection questions (Learning Edge)
if you decide it's relevant.

Lifelong Leadership Lessons

Questions for Reflection

Step Three: Now that you have placed all of the events onto your Leadership Plot Line, take time to think about the events and then step back to see how they connect through the patterns and themes.

Individual Events

- Think about all of the jobs you have held and the events on your map. What connects or links them? Why did you take the job, why did you leave? What mattered most to you in each job?

- What other experiences were you having just before, after, or during these events that had an influence on what you did or did not do?

- Reflecting on the painful or low points where you felt powerless, unseen, excluded, or put down, what was the key learning and its connection to the next high point?

- What moments were you the most courageous as you met challenges and how did this impact the outcomes and people closest to you?

Go Deeper

Values work: add to your values vocabulary by using a comprehensive values map. A larger vocabulary will aid in your ability to identify and therefore select preferred values as well as values based behaviors.

The Big Picture

- Were there times along this pathway that you stepped out of the action – what did you do and what was it that you valued most about these moments of stepping away from the path you were on at that time?

- How have these events or important people on your path formed your ideas, opinions, assumptions, and beliefs about leadership?

- How have all of these events and people in your life shaped your leadership style, e.g., fast paced, thoughtful, flexible, etc.?

What I Stand For

- Which of your beliefs inspire the strongest emotions?

- When have you made a difference – your words, actions, support, or sponsorship?

- What would make you change a belief? Do you think that changing a belief is considered dishonest?

- Do you believe you can make a difference in ways you have not, up to now? How? Where?

- If you had limiting beliefs about leadership, what might they be?

- What evidence, even slight, might be counter to these beliefs?

My Learning Edge (How might you be shaped by events in the future?)

- What leader do you think you are becoming? What do you aspire to be as a leader?

- As you understand the challenges and opportunities ahead, how do you think you might be impacted and changed by these challenges?

- How can you have others help one another to realize our ideal selves?

Lifelong Lessons Exercise

Step Four: Think about the most important experiences, influences, and events from the reflection work so far and list them below, filling in the details required by the template. Be sure to include events, even if brief or small, if they align with the leader you want to be.

EXPERIENCE (with key details such as time, place, emotions)	LESSONS LEARNED (what the event or person taught me)	PRIORITY VALUES (how you will see that event guide my behavior)
Example: *When I was 11, my father lost his business. He never gave up and rebuilt his business in a new city. We suffered as a family, losing our house and being without him for a time but a few years later we were able to buy a new home.*	**Example:** *Failures teach you much more about how to be successful than success can. There is no shame in loss. Loss can bring positive things you would not have gotten if it were not for the loss – it can be very creative.*	**Example:** *Perseverance, hard work, gratitude & appreciation of family.*
Title: Failure is the best teacher.		
1.		
Title:		
2.		
Title:		
3.		

Construction – "Who am I?"

Now put all of these individual experiences into a full "Who am I?" narrative.

A Few Tips

- Be willing to iterate – get all the thoughts out and then go back to refine and polish what you have written. Try setting it aside for a day or two

  - Bring the events to life by "re-enacting" them with details about the place, what people said, the reactions you had – provide the detail that will give the listeners a sense of being there

  - Share early versions with people who have known you and were part of the experiences to get their reactions and more detail from their memories

Go Deeper

Personal narrative: explore and then subtly shift limiting or outdated personal narratives using approaches from narrative therapy. Surface taken-for-granted beliefs and discover overlooked positive exceptions to the accepted narrative in order to emphasize a preferred narrative.

A strong "Who Am I?" story can use one of these themes from the bigger plot lines of life:

- Voyages and Return: Lessons learned that were repeated and reinforced over time

- The Quest or The Challenge: Obstacles and challenges overcome that changed you

- Mentors: Someone who inspired and invested in you

- Helpers: Advice from a wise person in your life

- Rags to Riches: Unexpected opportunities that transform our circumstances

- Overcoming Monsters: Mistakes and failures – learning the hard way

What to avoid:

- Preaching

- Talking down

- Sarcasm or negative comments

- Self-serving comments or "puffing yourself up"

Who I Am Today

How has your past shaped who you are as a leader? What challenges have you met, what choices did you make and why? What outcomes did you influence and how has this changed you?

Writing the "Who Am I?" Story

The Situation: What is your read of the current situation and what does the situation require of you now? Why? What is it about the current situation that is calling forth a specific life lesson or personal value? What about your experience enables you to meet the needs, as you see them? What can people count on from you? What do you expect from others and why?

_____

_____

_____

_____

_____

_____

_____

_____

_____

_____

What am I becoming that will be aided by the possibilities and challenges to come? How will I/we be changed by what lies ahead?

....

....

....

....

....

Go Deeper

Speech Acts: apply the insights from linguists that define a leader's speech as a set of discrete "acts." Know what these acts are to be precise in your use of them.

What, if any, call to action do you have for your audience that ties to your own personal story?

....

....

....

....

....

Take all of the elements from pages 25-27 and put them into a first draft of your narrative.

Steve Jobs' Stanford Commencement Speech, 2005

www.youtube.com/watch?v=UF8uR6Z6KLc

This speech shows how Steve Jobs' life experiences guided him to be the powerful influence he was to so many. This speech has been viewed over 15 million times.

© Matthew Yohe

I am honored to be with you today at your commencement from one of the finest universities in the world. I never graduated from college. Truth be told, this is the closest I've ever gotten to a college graduation. Today I want to tell you three stories from my life. That's it. No big deal. Just three stories.

The first story is about connecting the dots.

I dropped out of Reed College after the first 6 months, but then stayed around as a drop-in for another 18 months or so before I really quit. So why did I drop out?

It started before I was born. My biological mother was a young, unwed college graduate student, and she decided to put me up for adoption. She felt very strongly that I should be adopted by college graduates, so everything was all set for me to be adopted at birth by a lawyer and his wife. Except that when I popped out they decided at the last minute that they really wanted a girl. So my parents, who were on a waiting list, got a call in the middle of the night asking: "We have an unexpected baby boy; do you want him?" They said: "Of course." My biological mother later found out that my mother had never graduated from college and that my father had never graduated from high school. She refused to sign the final adoption papers. She only relented a few months later when my parents promised that I would someday go to college.

And 17 years later I did go to college. But I naively chose a college that was almost as expensive as Stanford, and all of my working-class parents' savings were being spent on my college tuition. After six months, I couldn't see the value in it. I had no idea what I wanted to do with my life and no idea how college was going to help me figure it out. And here I was spending all of the money my parents had saved their entire life. So I decided to drop out and trust that it would all work out OK. It was pretty scary at the time, but looking back it was one of the best decisions I ever made. The minute I dropped out I could stop taking the required classes that didn't interest me, and begin dropping in on the ones that looked interesting.

It wasn't all romantic. I didn't have a dorm room, so I slept on the floor in friends' rooms, I returned coke bottles for the 5¢ deposits to buy food with, and I would walk the 7 miles across town every Sunday night to get one good meal a week at the Hare Krishna temple. I loved it. And much of what I stumbled into by following my curiosity and intuition turned out to be priceless later on. Let me give you one example:

Reed College at that time offered perhaps the best calligraphy instruction in the country. Throughout the campus every poster, every label on every drawer, was beautifully hand calligraphed. Because I had dropped out and didn't have to take the normal classes, I decided to take a calligraphy class to learn how to do this. I learned about serif and san serif typefaces, about varying the amount of space between different letter combinations, about what makes great typography great. It was beautiful, historical, artistically subtle in a way that science can't capture, and I found it fascinating.

None of this had even a hope of any practical application in my life. But ten years later, when we were designing the first Macintosh computer, it all came back to me. And we designed it all into the Mac. It was the first computer with beautiful typography. If I had never dropped in on that single course in college, the Mac would have never had multiple typefaces or proportionally spaced fonts. And since Windows just copied the Mac, it's likely that no personal computer would have them. If I had never dropped out, I would have never dropped in on this calligraphy class, and personal computers might not have the wonderful typography that they do. Of course it was impossible to connect the dots looking forward when I was in college. But it was very, very clear looking backwards ten years later.

Again, you can't connect the dots looking forward; you can only connect them looking backwards. So you have to trust that the dots will somehow connect in your future. You have to trust in something – your gut, destiny, life, karma, whatever. This approach has never let me down, and it has made all the difference in my life.

My second story is about love and loss.

I was lucky – I found what I loved to do early in life. Woz and I started Apple in my parents' garage when I was 20. We worked hard, and in 10 years Apple had grown from just the two of us in a garage into a $2 billion company with over 4000 employees. We had just released our finest creation – the Macintosh – a year earlier, and I had just turned 30. And then I got fired. How can you get fired from a company you started? Well, as Apple grew we hired someone who I thought was very talented to run the company with me, and for the first year or so things went well. But then our visions of the future began to diverge and eventually we had a falling out. When we did, our Board of Directors sided with him. So at 30 I was out. And very publicly out. What had been the focus of my entire adult life was gone, and it was devastating.

I really didn't know what to do for a few months. I felt that I had let the previous generation of entrepreneurs down – that I had dropped the baton as it was being passed to me. I met with David Packard and Bob Noyce and tried to apologize for screwing up so badly. I was a very public failure, and I even thought about running away from the valley. But something slowly began to dawn on me – I still loved what I did. The turn of events at Apple had not changed that one bit. I had been rejected, but I was still in love. And so I decided to start over.

I didn't see it then, but it turned out that getting fired from Apple was the best thing that could have ever happened to me. The heaviness of being successful was replaced by the lightness of being a beginner again, less sure about everything. It freed me to enter one of the most creative periods of my life.

During the next five years, I started a company named NeXT, another company named Pixar, and fell in love with an amazing woman who would become my wife. Pixar went on to create the world's first computer animated feature film, Toy Story, and is now the most successful animation studio in the world. In a remarkable turn of events, Apple bought NeXT, I returned to Apple, and the technology we developed at NeXT is at the heart of Apple's current renaissance. And Laurene and I have a wonderful family together.

I'm pretty sure none of this would have happened if I hadn't been fired from Apple. It was awful tasting medicine, but I guess the patient needed it. Sometimes life hits you in the head with a brick. Don't lose faith. I'm convinced that the only thing that kept me going was that I loved what I did. You've got to find what you love. And that is as true for your work as it is for your lovers. Your work is going to fill a large part of your life, and the only way to be truly satisfied is to do what you believe is great work. And the only way to do great work is to love what you do. If you haven't found it yet, keep looking. Don't settle. As with all matters of the heart, you'll know when you find it. And, like any great relationship, it just gets better and better as the years roll on. So keep looking until you find it. Don't settle.

My third story is about death.

When I was 17, I read a quote that went something like: "If you live each day as if it was your last, someday you'll most certainly be right." It made an impression on me, and since then, for the past 33 years, I have looked in the mirror every morning and asked myself: "If today were the last day of my life, would I want to do what I am about to do today?" And whenever the answer has been "No" for too many days in a row, I know I need to change something.

Remembering that I'll be dead soon is the most important tool I've ever encountered to help me make the big choices in life. Because almost everything – all external expectations, all pride, all fear of embarrassment or failure – these things just fall away in the face of death, leaving only what is truly important. Remembering that you are going to die is the best way I know to avoid the trap of thinking you have something to lose. You are already naked. There is no reason not to follow your heart.

About a year ago I was diagnosed with cancer. I had a scan at 7:30 in the morning, and it clearly showed a tumor on my pancreas. I didn't even know what a pancreas was. The doctors told me this was almost certainly a type of cancer that is incurable, and that I should expect to live no longer than three to six months. My doctor advised me to go home and get my affairs in order, which is doctor's code for prepare to die. It means to try to tell your kids everything you thought you'd have the next 10 years to tell them in just a few months. It means to make sure everything is buttoned up so that it will be as easy as possible for your family. It means to say your goodbyes.

I lived with that diagnosis all day. Later that evening I had a biopsy, where they stuck an endoscope down my throat, through my stomach and into my intestines, put a needle into my pancreas and got a few cells from the tumor. I was sedated, but my wife, who was there, told me that when they viewed the cells under a microscope the doctors started crying because it turned out to be a very rare form of pancreatic cancer that is curable with surgery. I had the surgery and I'm fine now.

This was the closest I've been to facing death, and I hope it's the closest I get for a few more decades. Having lived through it, I can now say this to you with a bit more certainty than when death was a useful but purely intellectual concept:

No one wants to die. Even people who want to go to heaven don't want to die to get there. And yet death is the destination we all share. No one has ever escaped it. And that is as it should be, because Death is very likely the single best invention of Life. It is Life's change agent. It clears out the old to make way for the new. Right now the new is you, but someday not too long from now, you will gradually become the old and be cleared away. Sorry to be so dramatic, but it is quite true.

Your time is limited, so don't waste it living someone else's life. Don't be trapped by dogma – which is living with the results of other people's thinking. Don't let the noise of others' opinions drown out your own inner voice. And most important, have the courage to follow your heart and intuition. They somehow already know what you truly want to become. Everything else is secondary.

When I was young, there was an amazing publication called The Whole Earth Catalog, which was one of the bibles of my generation. It was created by a fellow named Stewart Brand not far from here in Menlo Park, and he brought it to life with his poetic touch. This was in the late 1960's, before personal computers and desktop publishing, so it was all made with typewriters, scissors, and polaroid cameras. It was sort of like Google in paperback form, 35 years before Google came along: it was idealistic, and overflowing with neat tools and great notions.

Stewart and his team put out several issues of The Whole Earth Catalog, and then when it had run its course, they put out a final issue. It was the mid-1970's, and I was your age. On the back cover of their final issue was a photograph of an early morning country road, the kind you might find yourself hitchhiking on if you were so adventurous. Beneath it were the words: "Stay Hungry. Stay Foolish." It was their farewell message as they signed off. Stay Hungry. Stay Foolish. And I have always wished that for myself. And now, as you graduate to begin anew, I wish that for you.

Stay Hungry. Stay Foolish.

Thank you all very much.

Delivery & Impact – "Who am I?"

Getting Feedback

First, share your stories with supportive allies. Then share them with progressively more critical allies. Be sure to include people who can provide insight into how the stories would be received in your organization.

Be clear on what feedback you would like each person to provide. Ask for feedback on not just the story content but also on how the story impacted the person and how well you told the story. Ask if they can reflect back the values that they think came across in the story.

Storytelling needs story listening. By hearing back what was heard, you can improve your storytelling capability.

Exercise

What feedback was most useful?

What Did I Learn?

Often, telling our life stories can have as big an impact on the author as it does on those listening.

- What were some of the insights gained from telling the story and seeing how it affected others? What impact did that have on you?

- What assumptions were challenged and which ones were confirmed about the impact of telling your personal stories?

- What did you learn about yourself that you were not aware of prior to the telling of the story?

Exercise

Write down impressions, insights, and responses to the questions provided.

Tracking Impact

The following suggestions can help you track the impact of your "Who Am I?" story.

- Ask for feedback from trusted peers, your boss, HR and OD professionals on your staff.

- Build in the opportunity to ask for feedback in one on one's with your subordinates and skip level subordinates on a regular basis.

- Provide methods for collecting feedback on your performance which are anonymous and technically up to date, i.e., Friday Fives, social software platforms, surveys, etc.

- Tell your "Who am I?" story regularly to reinforce the intent of being seen as approachable and real. Regular telling of your personal stories of challenges, learning, and celebration of your limitations provides the psychological safety needed to encourage others to share and learn from mistakes and errors.

"Stories we tell about our core values gain power in the retelling. Each time the story is retold the values that the story holds becomes more fully rooted within us."

– John Medina
Brain Rules

co-creation

community

identity

values

culture

Writing the "Who are we?" Narrative

Guiding Culture Change

"A story can alter the way we imagine ourselves and our worlds."

– Kendall Haven, "Story Proof" 2010

Introduction – "Who are we?"

Using the "Who are we?" narrative, a leader can describe the organization's identity. For that narrative to be truly compelling, a leader paints a picture that people can see themselves stepping into – a world that helps them see themselves as vibrant, multi-dimensional actors.

The "Who are we?" narrative is co-authored with the organization's members. Any identity narrative is already alive and well as a natural outcome of the storytelling being social. Among these stories is a dominant or shared narrative binding a culture together, for effective or ineffective outcomes. The more cohesive and positive the narrative, the more effective the organization will be because its members share an understanding of who they are, what actions their world requires of them, and what their purpose is.

The team, group or organization's shared reality is what participants agree it is. If an organization is to function optimally, which means leveraging culture in a way that ensures success, there must be some degree of consensus about the current and emergent reality. Shared reality, therefore, is not waiting to be discovered but is waiting to be invented.

The leader's work is to bring people together in a shared "Who are we?" narrative. This begins with hearing and collecting the current stories that people are telling, then the leader can better understand people's widely accepted set of assumptions and beliefs.

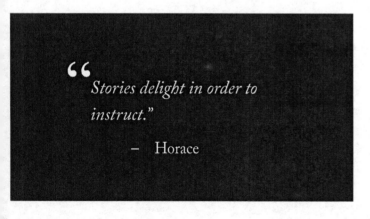

"
Stories delight in order to instruct."

– Horace

Once a comprehensive "Who are we?" narrative is constructed from the collection process, a leader can use their position power to institute methods for teams and the organization to reach consensus about what is real. This regular process of sharing their interpretation of events is also critical to the Strategic Narrative process covered in the next section.

To develop a co-created narrative through ongoing interpretation processes, gathering information about the culture must be institutionalized. Armed with a solid framework to accurately diagnose and assess the organization, a leader will obtain what is needed to construct – alone or with others – the "Who are we?" narrative. Ideally using a tool and process that can be repeated yearly.

The emphasis of the following section will be on how a leader prepares a "Who are we?" narrative.

Reflection – "Who are we?"

Using a Practical Model of Culture

A leader will need a comprehensive model for culture that can also act as a diagnostic tool. Understanding the current state and reflecting on the right stories to use for the "Who are we?" narrative are outputs of this in-depth process. A useful model will accelerate the discovery process and narrow down the areas that are the most important for the leader's focus.

The following model is based on what experts in the field of organizational culture and strategic planning have indicated are the observable manifestations of a culture. The connectors for all of these elements are the stories we tell about them.

Stories as the Connector

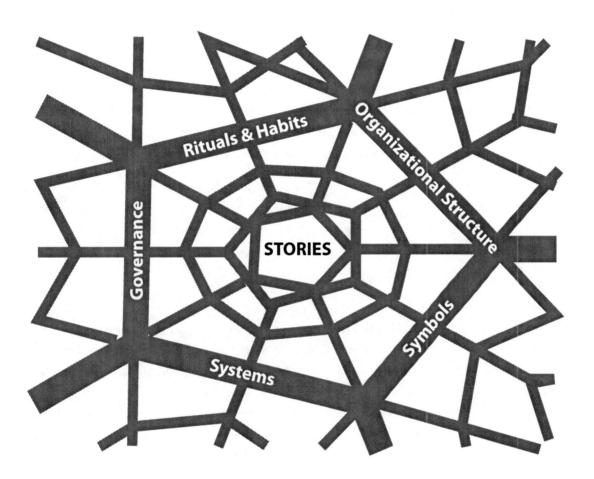

Stories as the Connector

There is a moment to moment influence on behaviors within an organization that can often be traced back to the stories being told within the organization. Stories tell us what people see as accurate and true about the organization. Often, the symbols, rituals, and habits one observes will be explained by the current stories. A leader can be listening for the words and metaphors chosen to tell the stories which gives insight to the interpretation of key events.

Stories to look for are accounts of past events and people who have been part of the successes or failures as the organization moves toward the stated goals. Who and what an organization's members choose to focus on says a great deal about what they value and what they perceive as both desired and out of bounds behavior. It's also important to note that the process of storytelling and the impact of new stories is interconnected and therefore always in flux.

The shared stories become a "story world" which captures what the majority of individuals in the organization agree is real. To fully grasp the import of the stories, it's critical to tap into all story sources; written histories, informal sources such as social media or rogue websites, your intranet, etc.

The five other elements are:

1. **Organizational Structure** – Structure is typically understood by looking at the organization chart. This document can give insight into how power and decision making is ideally or thought to be distributed. The concept of the organizational structure will provide a great deal of insight about the assumptions held by those in power about how an organization should function. Function follows design and the design is a cognitive model for beliefs about what should work. Inquiry would include evidence and the purpose of any alternative or informal structures.

2. **Governance** – It is governance within that structure that reveals who actually decides what and how. This is where the real power in the company resides vs. where the organization's design indicates the decision rights should exist. Governance is also reflective of adaptability, which is driven by the ability to learn as much as by the need to solve problems that surface.

3. **Systems** – These are the ways the organization is managed for consistency and predictability. They include: financial systems, quality systems, supply chain management, compensation, and rewards, including the way they are measured and distributed. This is where breakdowns occur when there are inconsistencies between governance, habits, and/or structure.

4. **Rituals and Habits** – It is the daily behavior and actions of people that signal acceptable behavior. This determines what is expected in given situations, and what is valued by management. Examples can be the number of hours expected of new associates to put in or the use of vacation time. These are typically captured in the messages given to new people coming into the organization or the patterns of behavior observed by those who are seen as models. They are on display and easily observed, even if they are not talked about openly.

5. **Symbols** – The visual representations of the company including logos, how sparse or plush the offices, Blackberry vs. iPhone, who sits where, posters on the wall, cafeterias, amenities provided to the employees, office layout and design, and the formal or informal dress codes.

Analyzing the "As Is" Culture

Start by gathering stories about the past as well as the stories people tell about the direction and purpose of the organization. You can then follow up by asking about the other five elements one by one, finishing with questions to determine consistencies and conflicts within each aspect of the culture.

Use this repetitive structure of inquiry:

- Tell me about something you experienced or witnessed that is an example of _____ .

- Share with me an anecdote or short story that describes why this is important.

  - What meaning do you take from this story, experience, observation?

  - To what degree do you believe others share this same interpretation of the event? How do you know this?

Mindset matters, so try to leave behind any preconceived ideas about the culture and set aside what culture work may be needed. Develop a theory about which part of the culture is strong or which aspect is experiencing the greatest disequilibrium, but it is recommended that a leader cast their net wide before coming to any conclusions about something as interconnected as culture.

Go Deeper

Culture measurement: use tested tools such as the Denison Culture Survey to collect data about your organization. The data can provide a starting point to construct the "Who are we?" story, especially in situations where the leader is new to the organization.

Initial Story Gathering

What historical events are known and discussed or kept alive over time?

_____

_____

_____

_____

Go Deeper

Story collection: tested methods and templates can assist a leader in mining and building a bank of stories. The organization needs a structured venue for storytelling and the interpretation process. This process of listening to the ever emerging stories in the organization is critical for change adoption.

What stories do people currently tell about the organization? (website/intranet, press, investment community, blogs, maverick websites, tweets)

_____

_____

_____

What reputation is communicated by your customers and other stakeholders? What do these stories say about what your organization believes in?

_____

_____

_____

What events do employees talk about when they think of the history of the company? What inspires you to come to work every day?

_____

_____

_____

What stories are told to new people who join the company? What heroes, villains, and mavericks appear in these stories? Are they different or one and the same?

_____

_____

_____

What example, no matter how small, shows a capacity to meet today's challenges?*

_____

_____

_____

_____

* Note: See more questions of this type on page 58.

Something to Be Aware Of

The simple act of asking the questions on pages 48-56 can help you create positive emotions and effects within the organization. This process alone can help to reinforce the positive identity of team members.

Genentech/Roche has done a superior job of connecting their employees, no matter what they do, to the positive impacts of saving lives with their drugs.

www.gene.com/gene/careers/employee_profiles.html

> "We take on characteristics in the stories we hear. We do this to see what the story reveals to us about the values hidden in the stories."
>
> – Lisa Cron
> *Wired for Story*

Organizational Structure

Is the structure flat or hierarchical? Formal or informal?

_____

_____

_____

_____

Where are the formal lines of authority? Are there informal lines? If informal lines exist, why did they come into being?

_____

_____

_____

_____

What metaphors do people use to describe the structure or design of the organization?

_____

_____

_____

_____

What do people believe this structure is designed to do as a means to achieving the desired results?

_____

_____

_____

_____

How does the structure ensure that accountability, team orientation, and skill meet the goals?

....

....

....

Governance

Who gets to decide what and when? Is that predictable? What isn't predictable? Why?

....

....

....

Who can change the rituals and habits? Which are problematic and why?

....

....

....

Who has the real power in the organization? What tells you that?

....

....

....

Who makes or influences decisions? How is this power used in intended or unintended ways?

What are, if any, the primary triggers for decision making about plans, strategies, and change in priorities? How do the problems surface? When and why?

How does the organization learn – from mistakes, from customers, from change?

Systems

- Planning Cycles
- Finance
- Performance Management
- Compensation
- Production
- Sales
- Communications – Marketing
- Organizational Development – Change Management

What process or procedure has the strongest controls? Weakest controls? (Prompt using the list above.)

_____

_____

_____

_____

Is the company, overall, loosely or tightly controlled?

_____

_____

_____

_____

How is the work measured and are the standards clear, fair, and appropriate? Do employees get rewarded for good work or penalized for poor work? Is this balanced?

_____

_____

_____

_____

What reports are issued to keep control of the systems?

_____

_____

_____

How is information distributed and shared across the organization?

_____

_____

_____

Has there ever been a crisis and how was that handled?

_____

_____

_____

How are changes managed – introduction of new systems, products, services as well as removing or stopping past systems/processes, products, services, etc.?

Rituals and Habits

What can customers expect when they interact with part of the organization?

What treatment do employees expect as they go about their work?

What would be noticed right away if a habitual way of doing things were to be changed to the good or to the detriment of our own stated goals?

What behaviors do these routines encourage?

_____

_____

_____

When a new problem is encountered, what rules do people apply when they solve it? What core beliefs do these rituals reflect?

_____

_____

_____

How are meetings, town halls, investor communications structured and performed?

_____

_____

_____

How similar or dissimilar are the experiences of people at each level of the organization **and** is leadership able to describe these various experiences in vivid detail?

_____

_____

_____

What new routines have been introduced and failed? What habits were in tension with this new routine? What new routines have been introduced and adopted with ease?

Symbols

Is company-specific jargon or language used? What terms are very meaningful to only those within the organization?

What metaphors are most often used to describe the organization?

How do people dress? Are the expectations for dress different at different levels of the organization?

_____

_____

_____

_____

What amenities are available, such as gyms and concierge services, day care, cafeterias? When are they open and are they subsidized?

_____

_____

_____

_____

Go Deeper

Organizational Stories: changing the organization's "taken for granted" stories to a deliberately selected preferred narrative may require assistance to guide a team or organization through this process.

What are the status symbols? (Placement of offices, size of offices, dress, use of or access to technology, perks, etc.)

_____

_____

_____

What images are associated with the organization, looking from the outside in or from the viewpoints of clients and vendors?

_____

_____

_____

_____

Be sure to document any questions used that are not part of those suggested.

Construction – "Who are we?"

Writing the "Who are we?" Story

Melding Many Stories into One Story

Understanding the cultural identity of any organization requires close observation and measured interpretation. Dedicating sufficient time to the process is critical to ensuring that the leader is able to not only hear all of the voices clearly but then blend the many stories into one.

The following process can guide a leader to prepare an effective "Who are we?" story.

1. **Analyzing Your Results** – The "as is" State

    As you interview people and collect the stories, you will start to build a picture, piece by piece, of what is influencing the culture. The next step is to integrate the various themes into a complete picture of the culture and make some generalized statements about "Who are we?," "Where did we come from?," and "Who are we becoming?" Using the stories and personal insights on an idea board can be a good start. Don't worry about sequencing, just select the best anecdotes and observations.

    When delivering the "Who are we?" narrative, you will speak for yourself and speak for others. Blending these two perspectives is important and requires personal clarity about the difference.

2. **Analyzing Culture** – The "to be" State

Starting with your organization's strategy as the rationale for emphasis, think about how you and others want the organization's ideal culture to look. To be believable by those in the organization, it is best to use positive aspects of the "as is" state to bridge into the aspirational or "to be" state. Use examples of how the future is alive today from your interviewing process. Here are some questions to gather examples of the organization at it's best.

- What have we done together in the past that helped us overcome what seemed like insurmountable obstacles?

- What example, no matter how small, shows a capability to face our challenges?

- How have we changed the world in a positive way, no matter how small?

- What makes us feel good about ourselves when we come to work?

- What values that matter have you demonstrated when you have a great day at work?

Go Deeper

Metaphors and Language: when the organization is large, multi-cultural, and new to the leader, guidance on how to link word and metaphor selection to the organization's values, beliefs, and cognitive models can accelerate the interpretation process.

3. **Mapping the Differences Between the Two** – Bridge "as is" to "to be"

The final product should:

- Identify the dominant aspects of the culture through anecdotes that reflect the identity of the organization.

- Describe the culture using a vocabulary that captures the priority values, whether they are lived or an aspiration. Typically, aspirations are alive and on display, even if in a small way, and can be brought to light by the leader. A powerful "Who are we?" story can actually bring out hidden patterns and new meaning. Taking scattered events and putting them into a coherent whole can emphasize a part of the organization's overlooked capacity for meeting the new challenges.

- Name things using new words that are positive and help people see themselves and the organization in new ways.

- Capture the most repeated stories as well as the rarer but powerful stories told by the organization's members, no matter the level or source. With a widely distributed organization, bringing in the voices from all corners of a global organization can reveal unseen points of alignment and diversity.

- Find thematic metaphors and stories associated with what is working and what is not. Do not flinch from speaking about the gaps. Bringing sensitivity to the way an issue is positioned while still naming the issue can provide a release of stress for those struggling under problems no one has named.

- Organize the stories into a coherent event line, taking the audience from the past to the present moments, challenges, and opportunities.

> "The notion of giving something a name is the vastest generative idea that was ever conceived."
>
> – Suzanne Langer, first female American philosopher

59

The Final Product

Use the following questions to construct your "Who are we?" narrative.

Where did we come from – what was the genesis of the organization?

_____

_____

_____

_____

What cultural strengths have been highlighted by your analysis? What makes us unique? What caused that uniqueness?

_____

_____

_____

_____

What has caused the current state of disequilibrium – what has or is going to change that will challenge the organization's identity? Introduce a theme, saying, or metaphor.

_____

_____

_____

_____

What cultural factors are hindering or are misaligned with the path forward?

_____

_____

_____

What part of the identity needs to be brought forward and reignited? How can we do that?

_____

_____

_____

What factors will you encourage and reinforce? What matters to you and why? Repeat the theme, saying, or metaphor.

_____

_____

_____

What needs to change? What new beliefs and behaviors do you need to promote? What evidence is there that proves "we can"? Why will this be hard or uncomfortable?

_____

_____

_____

_____

Go Deeper

TransMedia: deploying the "Who are we?" story for branding purposes may require an understanding of the various media you will use to tell your story. Facebook, LinkedIn, YouTube, websites, print ads, brochures need to tell the narrative in ways that are linked as well as appropriate to the medium/platform.

What is an inspirational summary? Repeat a theme, a saying, a metaphor.

_____

_____

_____

_____

Now take the key elements created on pages 60-62 and pull them together into a first draft. Use the following examples to think through how to refine your first draft.

Examples

"Working Together in the 21st Century"

Phil Condit, CEO Boeing
National Academy of Engineering
Frontiers of Engineering

September 18, 1997
Irvine, California

It is a great honor to stand before you, the "best of the best" of our young engineering community from industry, government, and academia. As an engineer and a member of NAE, I'm honored to be here.

Let me, first, congratulate you on your selection from 270 applicants to participate in NAE's Third Annual Frontiers of Engineering Symposium.

Secondly, I want to thank President Bill Wulf and the NAE for hosting this symposium, which allows you to find out about new research and pioneer thinking across many different fields. And you certainly are working on some exciting projects: biomechanics of cells and tissue engineering, optical filters, distributed satellite systems, ceramic sensors for automobiles, blended-wing-body aircraft concepts, neural networks, instrumentation for the evaluation of the lungs, and much more. This frontier symposium offers you great opportunity to learn and work together.

And since I do represent Boeing, I'm reminded that a symposium such as this simply can't take place without commercial airplanes. On average, 100,000 people are airborne on Boeing airplanes 24 hours a day, seven days a week. We move a lot of people. Airplanes allow us to get together to talk issues and dream… to forge new frontiers and make changes… to make the world a better place.

Tonight I'd like to spend some time talking about – recognizing change, the need to work together, and the ability to think differently about ourselves.

First, recognizing change.

We live in rapidly changing times. In just the last few months, NATO signed a new partnership agreement with its former Cold War adversary Russia, and Hong Kong reverted back to China. The Internet and CNN link us daily to other cultures and continents – even to outer space. Today we send mail electronically to each other and eye witness natural disasters and onboard space shuttle conversations – all from our homes. We live in a time of phenomenal change. We need to recognize this change.

I think it's critical to know it hasn't always been this way.

If you lived in medieval times, you would have little chance to change careers. You automatically did what your grandfather and father did, and your children followed – skills and crafts passed from generation to generation. In contrast, I believe people today can expect to make several dramatic career changes during their lifetime. Great change.

Likewise, people such as Benjamin Franklin, James Madison, and Alexander Hamilton probably traveled very slowly by horse-and-buggy to their convention to sign the U.S. Constitution just 219 years ago yesterday. In contrast, you quickly traveled many more miles to this symposium here in California – possibly by airplane.

Airplanes weren't even created 100 years ago, and the first artificial earth satellite, Sputnik, was only launched into orbit 40 years ago in 1957. Today, we watch a tiny vehicle chug around Mars on our television set or computer. Great change.

Technology and the world are changing at an outstanding rate. We have to keep up. Perpetuating "the status quo" in the future won't work.

So what are the implications of all this change for each of us? I think the implications are: either we must adapt to change or simply disappear. The Darwinian imperative says, "If we're unwilling to change, someone else will, and go forward."

Let me give you a couple of examples.

At the turn of the century, the seven largest national leather goods companies made buggy whips, saddles, and carriage seats. Because they failed to adapt when the motor car arrived, they don't exist today.

On the other hand, the Warren Featherbone Company, founded in 1883 in Michigan, does. They first recognized the need to replace more expensive whalebone used in women's corsets. They succeeded with turkey quills as a cheaper, more pliable stay material. Then, fashion changed. They had to adapt or be out of business. They moved to rubber diaper covers. Then, came disposable diapers. They learned to survive and thrive by reinventing and refocusing again. Today, they are a successful baby clothing manufacturer in Georgia.

At Boeing, I had to learn too. When I first came to Boeing in 1965, the biggest computer in the world couldn't compare to what I carry today in my briefcase. In the 1960's, airplanes were designed in pen and ink on big sheets of Mylar. Now our people create designs for airplane wings and parts on their computers. They work and rotate colorful, solid models to see all dimensions of their design. Great change.

We need to recognize and adapt to change.

Second, working together.

I happen to believe we control our own destiny, and that we can accomplish great things by working together.

Now I'm going to ask you to jump back in history one more time.

The Boeing Company was founded in 1916 by aviation pioneer Bill Boeing. He hired Tsu Wong, an engineering graduate from the Massachusetts Institute of Technology, to assist on the company's first airplane. During those early days of the company, employees sat together at the Red Barn, the company's first building in Seattle. Engineers upstairs; builders and accountants downstairs. All worked together side-by-side, solving daily problems.

So as the years rolled by, Boeing grew bigger. Bureaucracy crept in. Groups became isolated. The process became serial. And people did only their piece of the job and handed it over without sharing knowledge and resources. We were not lean and efficient.

When the idea of a whole new airplane family – the Boeing 777 – came along, we knew we had to do something different. The 777 has three million parts, stands six stories high, and uses 31,000 gallons of fuel. It has 2,885 pieces of tubing, 1,300 wire bundles, 14 tires, and two huge engines. To produce our new 777, it would take a new approach: a lot of people, and a lot of people working together.

We looked to those first days of our company and to our rich heritage to create the 777. And we began by creating a mission. Our mission statement became: Working Together to produce the preferred new airplane.

First, two key words, "Working Together."

As the 777 program started to develop, we said, "Let's invite our customers in; let's create teams to design and build our new airplane family; let's all work together."

Now none of us likes someone watching us. Others might find out our weaknesses. Might want to do our design work. Might try to take over. We had a lot of fear. But none of those fears came true.

A teacher friend of mine gave me a button a few years ago that read, "None of us is as smart as all of us." And I believe that statement is true. I also happen to believe it works well with the two words, "working together." We can do magical things working together.

In fact, our working together customers helped us with the 777. Helped a lot. Helped with the little things. Literally, thousands of things. Reading lights that can be easily changed in flight. Understanding that a latch, designed to be operated with a human finger, isn't a good idea with a glove on in minus 15 degrees at Chicago's O'Hare airport in January. I can go on and on.

We learned that it's worth your while to listen closely to the customer. The 777 is an airplane of thousands of "working together" ideas. Bottom line: working together worked.

Second, the next key word: Preferred.

Only the customer gets to decide what's "preferred." Preferred is a very strong reminder. We had a set of objectives to create the 777. And I got very excited at the first flight of the airplane a few years ago, and was asked "Why." I was excited because the process proved, "None of us is as smart as all of us." The bottom line: the process worked… not perfectly, but it worked.

Working together works. You can accomplish marvelous things.

Third, the ability to think differently about ourselves.

When I'm asked, "What's the most important thing you've learned in the last 10 years?" And I have to answer, "I can never say airplanes are different."

Learning to say that I'm not different; that my industry is not different; that my business is not different is hard. Airplanes are one of the best products in the world. They're a lot bigger. They're more complex. They fly. They are amazing machines.

By saying, "my business is different," is the best excuse for not learning. What you want to do is to learn from everyone. Your business isn't so special that you can't learn from anyone you meet.

I learned that while standing on the production line of Toyota, where I saw a very dramatic, efficient production system in Japan. I thought, "Interesting. But airplanes are different." The temptation is to say that, "They are very different." You produce at a different rate; your product is more complex; you have to be certified by the FAA. During that visit a few years ago, I learned that I was no longer allowed to say, "But we're different." Once we got over saying, "Airplanes are different," it improved the way we thought.

The ability to think differently about ourselves allows change.

And that brings me full circle.

First, the world is changing. Our choice is to recognize it is happening.

Second, working together is a powerful concept. None of us is as smart as all of us.

Third, we must start to think about ourselves differently.

I believe to survive in the 21st century, we must:

vow not to say that airplanes are different; engineers are different; doctors are different;

lawyers are different.

take as a motto: "Nothing endures but change."

we must adapt or disappear if we fall behind.

Every profession – whether it's engineering or medicine or law – is going to have to learn to adapt to a rapidly changing world.

Note: The following speech by Phil Condit has many of the same themes, but a very different audience. It is useful as an example of how language and stories subtly change based on the audience.

"Working Together to Create Better Cities"

Phil Condit, CEO Boeing
Asia Pacific Cities Summit

May 08, 2001
Seattle, Washington

It's great to be here tonight and to be able to share my views. But first, I want to congratulate all of you for coming together to discuss issues that face cities in this new century. Boeing is delighted to be a sponsor and to support a conference that brings people together to help solve common problems.

Tonight I want to talk about the benefits that might be derived from supporting growing cities in a rapidly changing, increasingly mobile society. I have a very fundamental premise that I want to offer: It is that economic growth follows infrastructure. If this premise is correct – I have heard it for many years, and I believe that it is – it leads to a critical conclusion: To have a strong, vibrant economy, a city needs a strong, integrated infrastructure. That means reliable, interdependent, efficient transportation and communications systems.

Let's look more closely at the premise that economic growth follows infrastructure. The great cities of the world grew up around access to transportation. Early in the history of the world's great cities, you didn't have to build transportation systems – it was the nearby rivers and oceans. So cities like Rome and Venice; London, Paris, and New York; Shanghai, Hong Kong, and Singapore; Seattle and Sydney all grew up around harbors for a good reason. For a brief period in the United States, some cities grew up around railroad transportation; Dallas/Fort Worth is a primary example. Today, air transportation is becoming increasingly critical for all cities. Orlando, Florida, for example, is experiencing amazing growth because of easy air access.

For vibrant cities, integrated air, sea, and land transportation systems will continue to be vital to economic growth. However, let me add one new challenge: this paradigm must include both transportation and communication systems, not as separate modes but as a complex, integrated set. One consideration to think about is the non-value-added travel time that impacts the movement of people and goods. The goods in a container on a ship are no more valuable after three days at sea than they were when they left. In fact, they may even be slightly less valuable because "time is money." Similarly, a passenger sitting idly in an airport waiting area is losing valuable time. Clearly, transporting people and goods will always involve non-value-added time, but technology offers many fascinating opportunities; e.g., technology can optimize the routing of goods in order to minimize transit time. Technology can allow the passenger in the waiting area to be on-line, doing something productive. By integrating systems together for the ease of the passenger or movement of products, people can be more productive and goods can be delivered faster. All this results in happier customers.

Let me give you a couple of examples – not real, but potential examples. A container ship crossing the Pacific Ocean is guided by GPS and, with the aid of satellite weather data, minimizes transit time. When the ship arrives at its destination port, both the shippers and customers receive an automatic status report as each container is off-loaded from the ship and loaded onto a train or truck. The trucks, carrying goods destined for another city, move away from the port on a dedicated right-of-way leading to the freeway system. This routing speeds travel and reduces congestion on surface streets. Trucks making local deliveries are guided by GPS along the optimum route to their destination. Trains leave the port on tracks that have no grade crossing, minimizing disruption to surface traffic. The combination of communications technologies and infrastructure design can dramatically speed the flow of goods and reduce the impact on the city.

I believe that there is an even more exciting possibility: air commerce. All of you who flew here probably had relatively similar travel experiences. But imagine if you could drive to the airport via easy freeway access and check-in using a fully electronic system; i.e., just wave your smart card, with its stored reservation, in front of a sensor. After you key in the number of bags that you are checking, the proper electronic bag strips appear, you attach them to your bags, place them on the conveyor, and then walk to the boarding area.

During the brief wait until boarding, you use your laptop and its wireless modem to watch the beginning of a critical sporting event and send a few e-mails. You board the plane – obviously, in this description, a new Boeing "Sonic Cruiser." After take-off, you pull out your laptop again and check the sporting event, using broadband wireless access provided by Connexion by Boeing. As the trip continues, you pay some bills, balance your bank account on-line, check on the stock market, and watch the end of the sporting event – all in real time.

The flight is guided by GPS in a new Air Traffic Management System that provides the flight crew guidance electronically, which allows more flights with greater safety and higher capacity in the system. Arrival is on-time, and your bags are waiting on the carousel when you reach it. You load them on a cart nearby and head down the escalator to the train station. (Yes, the cart has a rubber tread on the bottom to allow you to go up and down the escalator.) Once on the high-speed "city-link" train, you quickly check your wireless laptop for the market closing prices, then exit the train, and walk to your hotel, which is only two blocks from the station. The "wasted" time on this trip has been minimal. All of your e-mail is done, all your bills are paid, and your checking account is balanced. You are up-to-date on the news, you know who won the sporting event, and you are ready to go for a walk outside on the pleasant city streets before dinner.

Almost all of this is possible with technology available today. Some of you will have to wait for some of it, but with determination by cities and governments, it is possible. Easy access to airports by auto, light rail, and high-speed rail are a critical part. The incorporation of technology into passenger and baggage handling will take further investment, but the pay-off will be great. I believe this is the key: People migrate to systems that are convenient, economic, and reliable. Economies that have these attributes will be vibrant and growing.

I believe being mobile and connected also is changing the way we work and play. Being mobile and connected, for example, allows me to communicate better; in fact, a number of the tools I have talked about tonight I use on a regular basis. They allow me to meet more often with customers and with government and industry leaders, to see suppliers in person, and to visit employees wherever they work. Being mobile and connected allows me to answer e-mails, work on reports, look at data, and prepare and print a speech on a flight and deliver it an hour later. It has clearly changed the way I work. Being mobile and connected allows me to send e-mail directly to almost 160,000 Boeing employees from anywhere, at anytime. We are moving into a civilization that is linked by mobility and bandwidth and linked by integrated infrastructures. We are moving from a world marked by relative independence and one with real interdependence.

So I hope you believe my premise that economic growth follows infrastructure. If you believe that, then you must conclude that to have a strong, vital economy and growth in a rapidly changing world, cities will need a strong, integrated infrastructure. Cities will need good highway systems, good rail systems, and good airport systems – systems that are integrated and efficient. Cities will need good communications systems, which maintain high reliability... systems that are "always on."

I believe we can succeed in meeting the challenges of congestion, moving large volumes of freight and large numbers of passengers, and eliminating bottlenecks at airports and marine terminals. I believe we can meet the challenges of digital security and Internet privacy. I believe that we, as leaders – of cities, of corporations – play a unique leadership role in building the infrastructure foundation that must come first. We have a great opportunity to integrate land, air, and sea transportation. We have a great opportunity to connect and build communications systems that are more reliable, "always on."

We can act together to implement a vision. It means that we must be willing to think differently, be willing to imagine, be willing to innovate. It means that we must be willing to look at models that are different, models that work, and models that work in different places, and to imagine new models of infrastructure and new ways to integrate. There is, and will continue to be, resistance as we work through this great change, but we have choices. We can lead, move ahead, and embrace the future or try to hold back the inevitable advance of the tide. What most of us want is progress, but without change that will not happen.

Let me close with the words of Charles Darwin. I think they are very important. He said: "It is not the strongest of the species that survives nor the most intelligent; it is the one that is most adaptable to change." I think we can lead and survive and prosper by adapting and taking advantage of the great technology that is available to us. And I think we can make a difference.

Thank you.

Exercise

Reflect upon the questions provided. Write down what was most memorable about these narratives? Why?

- What were the themes?
- What would you say the values and assumptions are that this narrative highlights?
- What was Phil Condit asking people to do and why?
- How were the two narratives the same, different? Why, in your view?
- What ideas from reading these two speeches can you carry into your own "Who are we?" narrative?

Delivery & Impact – "Who are we?"

Delivery

Before

Before delivering the "Who are we?" narrative, a leader should socialize all or selected elements of the narrative. Be sure to involve others in the refinement of the final message.

Awareness of the symbolic meaning that people will infer from elements of the delivery such as timing, the physical place, and the artifacts or images used for the delivery of the narrative is critical. One sour note, such as picking a date or a location that has significance to the audience that is counter to the message, can be what comes through louder than the words. Cultural blind spots can be detrimental, so a leader should use credible and wise cultural guides as the plans are finalized and communicated.

During

All of the requisite platform skills for powerful delivery are important, but the most important element is the leader's conviction and full belief in what they are saying. Polished presentation skills are less important than genuine passion. It is harder to authentically speak for yourself **and** others than to only speak from personal experience and vision. This requires true empathy and the ability to talk about what matters to everyone else in the room.

(See pages 105-106 for additional thoughts about presentation skills.)

The concept of storytelling **and** story-listening as a complete cycle of communication is relevant when sharing the "Who are we?" narrative. Preparing for feedback, dialogue, and group interpretation of what has been heard extends the telling of the narrative out into a group process. Including a back and forth dialogue ensures that you build a shared meaning of the words.

Immediately After

Allowing for ongoing feedback and dialogue after the presentation is critical given that any organization has a combination of extroverted and introverted people. Introverted people require more time to process and the outputs of their reflection can be quite useful to the group's understanding of the narrative and its implications.

This dynamic process can be facilitated in a number of ways with social software platforms, intranets, or feedback mechanisms that send information up and down the organization.

Go Deeper

Platform skills: getting skilled coaching for public presentations can ensure that you are prepared for the venue on all levels; verbal skills, use of voice and body, effective audio/visual support, how to handle interviews with press, fielding questions, and video do's and don'ts.

Impact

Of the three, the "Who are we?" narrative is the broadest and most long lived narrative while also being the hardest to track in all of its shadings and evolution. It's wise to have a variety of ways to track impact.

Measurement

There are assessments available which can give leaders hard data on important cultural indices. The Denison Culture survey, based on the author's experience with a wide range of instruments, is likely the best available due to its reliable and valid normative data, clear and easy to understand language along with very direct links between observable behaviors and business results. The survey provides insight into employee engagement as part of a larger set of factors.

A good tool will allow you to collect data from your organization, formulate action plans, and then survey yearly to measure progress against the critical cultural indices which will drive the desired results. This is an instance where using professional support would be helpful to guide culture change efforts.

Ongoing Storytelling and Storylistening

Collecting and disseminating stories to strengthen and build the culture is a methodology used by some well know organizations such as Disney, Four Seasons Hotels & Resorts, and Haas Business School to name a few.

An integrated set of systems and processes can be instituted to firmly embed storytelling to guide people toward the desired behaviors.

transparency

words-are-worlds

self-knowledge

creation

authenticity

Writing the "Where are we going?" Narrative

Strategic Narrative

"Leaders think otherwise and take us elsewhere."

– Bob Galvin, CEO of Motorola 1958 - 1986

Introduction – "Where are we going?"

Narrative intelligence is an innately human ability to make sense of the world through storytelling. Applying this intelligence to the "Where are we going?" story is a critical tool that helps an organization to:

- strengthen organizational visions,

- enhance organizational communications,

- capture and transfer organizational knowledge,

- encourage innovation,

- build communities, and

- develop effective learning strategies.

Narratives and specific stories in the business environment can show up in a variety of forms; oral and written stories, videography/documentaries, oral histories, organizational myths and legends, long range strategic scenarios, business case scenarios, training scenarios, business rules, gossip, and business conversations.

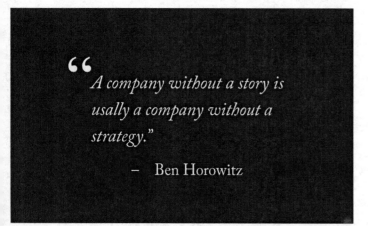

> "
> *A company without a story is usually a company without a strategy.*"
>
> – Ben Horowitz

This section of the guide will focus on the use of narrative structure to formulate and deliver the organization's strategy. You will be provided the steps for writing and gaining buy-in to the strategic narrative – the story of a path to success for the organization.

What Must a Strategic Narrative Do?

A Strategic Narrative is an imagined future captured in a "before," "now," "to be" sequence. This type of narrative sets the stage by informing the listener of relevant history and current conditions. It defines the challenges or opportunities to be addressed, and it describes how those challenges will be met. A Strategic Narrative "event line" establishes a fundamental understanding of actions to be taken in the face of a threat or opportunity.

An effective Strategic Narrative uses the economy of delivery a PowerPoint presentation provides without losing the complexity of meaning to guide purposeful and goal directed activity.

You know you have a good Strategic Narrative when it:

- Provides a plot line or "new story" to replace the old
- Provides new metaphors that influence focus and choices across all functions
- Instructs people on the steps to be taken – in ways that seem possible
- Clarifies the current challenges
- Engages and instructs others on how to access the competencies available in the face of new challenges
- Shows the way to new values while honoring the old ones
- Paints a picture of what success "looks like, feels like, tastes like"
- Inspires commitment to a course of action

Reflection – "Where are we going?"

Understanding the Current Landscape

Strategies must be adaptive to continuous change and responsive to current business conditions while still being specific about how to get there. Alan Webber of Fast Company calls this the balance of "tight and loose." It's a combination of listening to the marketplace and deep reflection on what we collectively believe to be real. This level of discussion and interpretation can, to some extent, anticipate the future from the patterns that emerge. A solid strategy is built upon credible content, and an Environment Scan helps build that content.

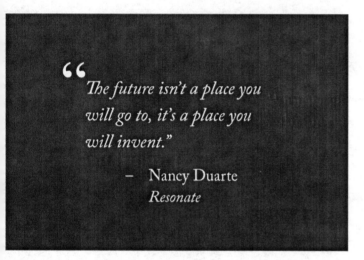

> " *The future isn't a place you will go to, it's a place you will invent.*"
>
> – Nancy Duarte
> *Resonate*

By definition, an Environment Scan is a review of anecdotes, data, voice of the customer outputs, research from industry experts, intelligence on your competition, and projections provided by internal experts on how the organization performs.

It is the dialogue, the interpretation, and sense making of all of these inputs, which is the most critical element of the Environment Scan process.

The following areas cover both external and internal environments relevant to building a strategy. Each organization has to select what fits from these "buckets" or add to this list.

1. Customers

2. Markets

3. Competition

4. Innovation

5. Quality

6. Goals – Scorecard, KPI, yearly objectives (commitments and requirements)

7. Initiatives (organizational priorities)

8. Financials (budgets, forecasts)

9. People

10. Community

How to Conduct an Environment Scan

When conducting Environment Scans the primary concern is to answer the following questions for each of the selected "buckets":

1. What do we know right now about _____ that affect the organization – internally and externally?

2. What do we suppose is just over the horizon?

3. How do **we** (collectively) know this and does it match the view of external constituents?

4. What will we select for our strategic focus from the information we have reviewed?

5. What do our choices reflect about our values and beliefs?

The following questions are provided to the team, along with any reading materials to review, prior to a one to two day group session.

Allowing enough time and providing guidelines for the inquiry will ensure that people come to the session prepared with new and fresh thinking.

Assigning the "buckets" of categories to small teams can also be effective, allowing several minds to go deep and leverage the collective thinking of the subgroups.

Specific questions will need to be formulated for fleshing out the current and future environment in each of the ten areas. Use the following questions as a starting point.

External

Customers/Stakeholders

- Who are our principle stakeholders, clients, customers, end-users?

- What is most important to who we serve, today? Tomorrow?

- How are we currently meeting their needs?

- How are we perceived by those we serve?

- What bargaining power do the people we serve have and how has that changed or could change?

Markets

- What are the most important global trends affecting our market today?

- What markets are dying? What future markets are emerging?

- Who are the new entrants?

- What substitutes for our services and products are emerging and why?

Competition

- What is the primary advantage of our competition today?

- What is the primary weakness?

- What changes in the competitive environment would favor our success?

- What is our reputation with our competitors?

Internal

Innovation

- How can we strengthen quality and innovation now and into the future?

- How well are we organized and resourced to enhance innovation?

  - What innovations are not funded/under-funded that could be future "bets" for us?

Quality

- How would customers describe our quality?

  - What are the most important quality issues for us?

  - What future requirements or changes in "inputs" to our product/service could negatively/positively impact our quality?

Goals

- What expectations must we fulfill – from the Board, from the organization as a whole, as part of my group's charter, etc.?

- What expectations may change or emerge in the next 3-5 years? What will that mean to our current goals?

- What commitments are the most challenging, motivating, problematic?

- Where are our priorities in conflict?

Initiatives

- What initiatives being driven in our organization or functional areas are impacting our organizational and local strategies?

- What impacts do we need to factor in as these initiatives roll out?

- How do these initiatives operationalize our priorities? What gaps exist between stated priorities and our initiatives?

Go Deeper

Voice of the Customer and Focus Groups: using tested methods for collecting customer and constituent feedback can best be accomplished by using the tools from the field of Corporate Anthropology.

Financials

- How well do we understand the financial situation, and how can we learn more?
- What financial changes do we anticipate for the organization and its functional groups?
  - What budget constraints might impact the strategy?
    - How will global markets and governmental actions impact our financial picture over the long term?

People

- Who in our network (team, peers, senior management, other internal organizations, customers, and vendors) trusts our organization?
  - With which members of our network (team, peers, senior management, customers, and vendors) do I need to build trust?
  - What cultural strengths do we have and how are they demonstrated? Where are the weaknesses?
  - What capabilities are differentiators? Should be differentiators?

Community

- What responsibilities to community are we fulfilling and how?
- Where are there unmet needs which we can fulfill in the spirit of enlightened self interest?

Go Deeper

Change Plans:
select and adapt a change management model.

Leading a Strategic Narrative Development Process

The following steps outline how to initiate and lead a Strategic Narrative development process.

1. Organize the Data

Building a Strategic Narrative is an iterative process. Many leaders have a daily discipline of collecting random thoughts, clippings, or sample narratives.

Gather the necessary data. Utilize the outputs of a personal or collective Environment Scan, which includes external as well as internal resources.

A Strategic Narrative should define resources available, constraints, organizational capabilities to be applied, and time priorities. A strong Strategic Narrative is data based but brings the data alive within a narrative structure that organizes disparate elements into a rationale for doing something different.

2. Compose a Strategic Narrative Event Line

The leader has to be clear on the intent of their message. Is it to inspire, influence, instruct, or a combination of these? The Event Line has to reflect the intention of the leader.

Using a simple time sequence of Past, Present, Future, segregate the various elements into the story sequence of a narrative. These segments have specific questions on the following pages. This detail will build the anchoring elements and themes into a logical flow.

Using a powerful new metaphor can unify a Strategic Narrative as well as inspire people to think about their organization in ways that break apart old assumptions. See the following exercise for how to engage others in the process of developing a metaphor for the future organization.

3. Engage Others

There are many ways and points along the way that others can be involved. Teams can build a Strategic Narrative together, start to finish. Some leaders tap into advisors, do test runs, or gather feedback on early iterations of the Strategic Narrative. These choices will be individual to each leader and situation.

The real work of leaders is to create and hold a vision of what the world or some part of it will be in the future. There are examples of visions which are largely from the mind of one leader, such as Larry Ellison of Oracle or Steve Jobs when he was alive. Once the kernel of the vision is articulated, leaders enroll others by matching a personal vision of success with the organization's shared aspiration. The majority of strategies that support these visions are typically formulated with a wider population of inputs and voices. Using this approach an individual leader can begin engaging others in building a more robust narrative.

Working With Metaphor

Metaphors are critical when developing strategies for change because they reveal the framework an individual or group uses to interpret events and decide what action to take. An individual makes sense of the world through an internal framework or conceptual system which is revealed through the words, phrases and metaphors of the language. Language is metaphorical in nature.

So as the Peter Block quote on page 1 says, "All change is linguistic," meaning change starts with our language. If a leader wants to change how people behave, start with the metaphors. They are not just a figure of speech.

Before introducing new metaphors, a leader will need to invest time in interviewing a cross section of employees, careful listening, and reading relevant documents. The leader will be looking for the metaphors that have the greatest meaning to the individuals in the organization. This meaning can translate into positive images and concepts that guide or even inspire action. You would want to keep or build on these. There are also metaphors which can limit thinking or action and keep the organization's members stuck in unproductive patterns. Often people are unaware of the negative impacts of these old metaphors. These are metaphors you would want to replace with new, positive metaphors.

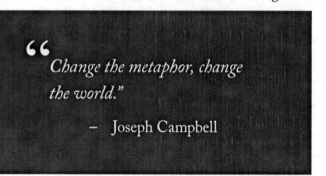

Change the metaphor, change the world."

– Joseph Campbell

The most effective metaphors are physically oriented. For example, the metaphor of "removing barriers" is far more impactful than "empower our people." This is because the act of removing a barrier is something we understand at a physical level and is easily seen in the mind's eye. Neuroscience research indicates that these types of metaphors are experienced as if we were actually performing the act. "Empowerment" is more abstract and can be interpreted in many different ways.

After a thorough investigation of what metaphors are currently being used, the leader can reinforce or build upon existing metaphors, and introduce a new metaphor to replace old ones. A leader will need to monitor the number of metaphors used to avoid confusion in the audience's mind. One of the reasons metaphors are particularly powerful is because they are mini stories unto themselves, conveying a rich set of meanings – and very quickly. So, less is more.

Leaders can guide discussions about metaphors that describe the current and desired state for the team or organization. This type of discussion can pave the way for a new and preferred narrative for change because speaking with metaphors makes it safe to discuss our hidden assumptions. Often it is the un-discussed or hidden beliefs that can trip up a team or organization. The use of a metaphor to talk about difficult subjects seems to work because it externalizes the issue instead of placing blame for problems on the people around the table. The following exercise will help a leader discuss even the most challenging subjects when it's important to speak honestly about an organization's current state before developing a strategy for change.

Exercise

One of the most effective ways to get people talking about their view of the organization is to have them use metaphors to describe the current state. This is particularly effective when the objective is to engage people while early in the process of building a new narrative. The outcome is a pivot off of the dominant metaphor(s) to create a new or preferred metaphor.

Step One: The first step is to invite participants to complete a sentence:

"If <our organization> was a <category> it would be a <example> because…" The category could be a mode of transport or a movie or a sport (real or imagined) or an animal.

"If <our organization> was an animal it would be a monkey because we're social and we are always jumping from idea to idea."

"If <our organization> was a mode of transport it would be a Bentley because our quality is excellent but maybe we're just a bit too comfortable."

The exercise can be done either individually or in pairs. If people work alone, ask them to write down or draw their answer. If people work alone it is important that they have time for discussion with others to draw out the "because."

Step Two: In the discussion, tacit dimensions of the organization become explicit and organizational values become evident. The exercise also allows people to surface un-discussables or sources of conflict with humor. The dangerous becomes safe.

Step Three: Now build on this exercise by asking people to talk about a metaphor that conveys an ideal state.

Step Four: Discuss how to bridge between the two states, current and "to be." Connect back into the process of developing the Strategic Narrative from this point in the discussion.

Go Deeper

Metaphors: professionals can facilitate the exploration of metaphors that resonate for a large, global and/or multi-cultural organization. Thoughtful selection of metaphors as well as the process of engaging people in coming up with guiding metaphors can benefit from corporate anthropological methods.

Writing the Event Line of a Strategic Narrative

A well written narrative has an event line that anchors all of the defining milestones in a time bound sequence; Past, Present, and Future. This structure mirrors the way we naturally package information for rapid comprehension and organization of multiple pieces of information. Writing a Strategic Narrative is intended to create a communication experience instead of a static message.

A leader has to first define the events along the path like the plot line of a novel. It is an iterative process, beginning with defining the events that anchor the narrative, start to finish. Once the anchoring events are chosen, detail and memorable elements can be added.

Where you've been	Where you are	Where you are going

Event Time Line →

Defining Events Along the Way

Read the sample Strategic Narrative on pages 96-97 and ask yourself, "What are the anchoring events in the Past, Present, and Future along the event line of the story?" Note the repetition of very specific themes and a clear call to action.

> " *Leaders live in the tension between what is and what could be. Their words are our bridge to the future.*"
>
> — Peter Senge

Construction – "Where are we going?"

Adding Detail to the Strategic Narrative Event Line

Use the following segmentation of the Strategic Narrative and the questions provided to build a first draft of the Strategic Narrative.

What are the Elements of a Strategic Narrative?

These three elements reflect the Past to Present to Future structure of any narrative.

I. Set the Stage

Reflect on what has already happened:

- Where are we today?
- How did we get here?
- What have we learned from the past?
- What happened in the past that shaped our identity?
- How did that form how we perceive ourselves?
- What matters to us within that identity?
- Why does it matter?

II. Define the Current Challenges & Opportunities

How do we see today?

- What turning point do we find ourselves having to address?
- What's holding us back?
- What's driving us forward?
- What are our most critical conflicts?
- How are we resolving these critical conflicts?
- What actions are important to take now?
- What roadblocks might we encounter along the way?
- What must we **start** doing?
- What must we **stop** doing?
- What will it take to win?

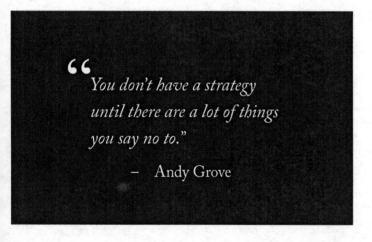

" *You don't have a strategy until there are a lot of things you say no to.*"

— Andy Grove

III. Describe the Resolution

What is our preferred future?

- What primary goal will be reached?
- Why is that important to us?
- How does it reflect who we are?
- What will it look, smell, taste, and feel like when we get there?
- What am I calling you to do?
- What will I commit to doing?
- What's in it for me, you, and all of us?
- How will we be changed for the better?

Examples

Internet Software Services

From: Bill Gates

Sent: Sunday, October 30, 2005 9:56 PM

To: Executive Staff and Direct Reports; Distinguished Engineers

Microsoft has always had to anticipate changes in the software business and seize the opportunity to lead.

Ten years ago this December, I wrote a memo entitled The Internet Tidal Wave which described how the internet was going to forever change the landscape of computing. Our products could either prepare for the magnitude of what was to come or risk being swept away. We dedicated ourselves to innovating rapidly and lead the way much to the surprise of many industry pundits who questioned our ability to reinvent our approach of delivering software breakthroughs.

Five years ago we focused our strategy on .NET making a huge bet on XML and Web services. We were a leader in driving these standards and building them into our products and again this has been key to our success. Today, over 92% of the Fortune 100 are utilizing .Net and our current wave of products have XML and Web services at their core and are gaining share because of the bold bet we made back in the year 2000.

Today, the opportunity is to utilize the Internet to make software far more powerful by incorporating a services model which will simplify the work that IT departments and developers have to do while providing new capabilities.

In many ways this is not completely new. All the way back in 1998 we had a company meeting where we outlined a vision in which software would become more of a service over time. We've been making investments since then – for example, the Watson service we have built into Windows and Office allows us and our partners to understand where our users are running into problems and lets us improve their experience. Our On-line help work gives us constant feedback about what topics are helping our users and which we need to change. Products from MSN like Messenger and Hotmail are updated with new features many times throughout the year, allowing them to deliver innovations rapidly. Our Mappoint service was a pioneer in letting corporations connect up to a web based API on a subscription basis.

However, to lead we need to do far more. The broad and rich foundation of the internet will unleash a "services wave" of applications and experiences available instantly over the internet to millions of users. Advertising has emerged as a powerful new means by which to directly and indirectly fund the creation and delivery of software and services along with subscriptions and license fees. Services designed to scale to tens or hundreds of millions will dramatically change the nature and cost of solutions deliverable to enterprises or small businesses.

We will build our strategies around Internet services and we will provide a broad set of service APIs and use them in all of our key applications.

This coming "services wave" will be very disruptive. We have competitors who will seize on these approaches and challenge us – still, the opportunity for us to lead is very clear. More than any other company, we have the vision, assets, experience, and aspirations to deliver experiences and solutions across the entire range of digital work style & digital lifestyle scenarios, and to do so at scale, reaching users, developers and businesses across all markets.

But in order to execute on this opportunity, as we've done before we must act quickly and decisively. This next generation of the internet is being shaped by its "grassroots" adoption and popularization model, and the cost-effective "seamless experiences" delivered through the intentional fusion of services, software and sometimes hardware. We must reflect upon what and for whom we are building, how best to deliver new functionality given the internet services model, what kind of a platform in this new context might enable partners to build great profitable businesses, and how our applications might be reshaped to create service-enabled experiences uniquely compelling to both users and businesses alike.

Steve and I recently expanded Ray Ozzie's role as CTO to include leading our services strategy across all three divisions. We did this because we believe our services challenges and opportunities will impact most everything we do. Ray has long demonstrated his passion for software, and through his work at Groove he also came to realize the transformative potential for combining software and services. I've attached a memo from Ray which I feel sure we will look back on as being as critical as The Internet Tidal Wave memo was when it came out. Ray outlines the great things we and our partners can do using the Internet Services approach.

The next sea change is upon us. We must recognize this change as an opportunity to take our offerings to the next level, compete in a manner commensurate with our industry responsibilities, and utilize our assets and our broad reach to reshape our business for the benefit of the users of our products, our customers, our partners and ourselves.

Bill Gates

Exercise

Before looking at the answers below, go back and see if you can determine where the Past, Present and Future oriented states are and then look for the anchoring events. After a second review, use the answers below to guide your learning.

Answers

Past, Present, and Future are separated in the large boxes, anchoring events are underlined.

PAST Microsoft has always had to anticipate changes in the software business and seize the opportunity to lead.

Ten years ago this December, I wrote a memo entitled The Internet Tidal Wave which described how the internet was going to forever change the landscape of computing. Our products could either prepare for the magnitude of what was to come or risk being swept away. <u>We dedicated ourselves to innovating rapidly and lead the way</u> much to the surprise of many industry pundits who questioned our ability to reinvent our approach of delivering software breakthroughs.

Five years ago we focused our strategy on .NET making a huge bet on XML and Web services. <u>We were a leader in driving these standards and building them into our products</u> and again this has been key to our success. Today, over 92% of the Fortune 100 are utilizing .Net and our current wave of products have XML and Web services at their core and are gaining share because of the bold bet we made back in the year 2000.

PRESENT Today, the opportunity is to utilize the Internet to make software far more powerful by incorporating a services model which will simplify the work that IT departments and developers have to do while providing new capabilities.

In many ways this is not completely new. All the way back in 1998 we had a company meeting where <u>we outlined a vision in which software would become more of a service</u> over time. We've been making investments since then – for example, the Watson service we have built into Windows and Office allows us and our partners to understand where our users are running into problems and lets us improve their experience. Our On-line help work gives us constant feedback about what topics are <u>helping our users</u> and which we need to change. Products from MSN like Messenger and Hotmail are updated with new features many times throughout the year, allowing them to <u>deliver innovations rapidly</u>. Our Mappoint service was a pioneer in letting corporations connect up to a web based API on a subscription basis.

FUTURE However, <u>to lead we need to do far more</u>. The broad and rich foundation of the internet will unleash a "services wave" of applications and experiences available instantly over the internet to millions of users. (PRESENT Advertising has emerged as a powerful new means by which to directly and indirectly fund the creation and delivery of software and services along with subscriptions and license fees.) Services designed to scale to tens or hundreds of millions will <u>dramatically change the nature and cost of solutions</u> deliverable to enterprises or small businesses.

<u>We will build our strategies around Internet services and we will provide a broad set of service APIs and use them in all of our key applications.</u>

This coming "services wave" will be very disruptive. <u>We have competitors who will seize on these approaches and challenge us – still, the opportunity for us to lead is very clear.</u> More than any other company, we have the vision, assets, experience, and aspirations to deliver experiences and solutions across the entire range of digital work style & digital lifestyle scenarios, and to do so at scale, reaching users, developers and businesses across all markets.

PRESENT/FUTURE PIVOT But in order to execute on this opportunity, as we've done before <u>we must act quickly and decisively</u>. This next generation of the internet is being shaped by its "grassroots" adoption and popularization model, and the cost-effective "seamless experiences" delivered through the intentional fusion of services, software and sometimes hardware. <u>We must reflect upon what and for whom we are building, how best to deliver new functionality given the internet services model, what kind of a platform in this new context might enable partners to build great profitable businesses, and how our applications might be reshaped to create service-enabled experiences uniquely compelling to both users and businesses alike.</u>

FUTURE Steve and I recently expanded Ray Ozzie's role as CTO to include leading our services strategy across all three divisions. We did this because <u>we believe our services challenges and opportunities will impact most everything we do.</u> Ray has long demonstrated his passion for software, and through his work at Groove he also came to realize the transformative potential for combining software and services. I've attached a memo from Ray which I feel sure we will look back on as being as critical as The Internet Tidal Wave memo was when it came out. Ray outlines the great things we and our partners can do using the Internet Services approach.

<u>The next sea change is upon us. We must recognize this change as an opportunity to take our offerings to the next level, compete in a manner commensurate with our industry responsibilities, and utilize our assets and our broad reach to reshape our business for the benefit of the users</u> of our products, our customers, our partners and ourselves.

Exercise

To build the events of the Strategic Narrative, answer the following questions:

Reflect on all of the data collected for the environment scan and analysis **before** proceeding. Once you are confident you have segregated down to the relevant inputs, begin by listing the anchoring events, Past & Present:

_____

_____

_____

_____

_____

What themes or patterns seem to cut across Past and Present? What themes do you want to emphasize?

_____

_____

_____

What future events or impacts do you envision that would be critical or indicate success?

_____

_____

_____

_____

Making the Message Memorable

Add Elements That Engage the Whole Person

A leader's audiences have to be identified so that the selection of messages, anecdotes, and supporting graphics will bring out the reactions desired. A good narrative must include elements that help the audience use their imagination and engage all of their physical senses. Metaphors, graphics, memorable statistics, surprising elements all work together to make the message memorable and meaningful.

Go over the first draft created by answering the questions provided on pages 93-95 and then use the following exercise to layer in language, anecdotes, statistics in these four areas: Reason, Emotion, Imagination, and the 5 Senses.

Reason

How do you appeal to people's logic and intelligence?

- Powerful statistics and facts are necessary to present a credible case for change.

- People can remember up to three important facts, plus or minus one. Use them sparingly. Think 3's – no more than three facts, three themes, three questions…

- Frame questions for people to think about – don't give too much detail.

Emotion

How do you know what emotions people are feeling (or want to feel) and acknowledge, evoke, or mirror these emotions?

- Know the emotions that may be currently the most prevalent among your audience. If you do not speak to these emotions first, you cannot move people to new actions.

- Know how to describe the culture in familiar terms. Connect them to the "Who are we?" story in a way that is meaningful and therefore emotion laden.

- Know the most highly held values – those in actual use and those that are aspirational – link them to the desired behaviors, make them the hero in the story.

- Be aware of the current environmental influences and the impact anxiety, stress, or fear may be having on your audience. Speak to the key conflicts that define the journey.

- Be able to speak to why they work for the company and what the global goal may be.

- Share compelling anecdotes that personalize a point – dissatisfaction is just a concept until the listener is brought to a reenactment of an event that caused dissatisfaction.

Imagination

How do you seed new thoughts in people's minds?

- Stay in the near future – don't go out too far.

- Build out from something known into something unknown. Look for an event that will help people see how the change desired for the future may already exist in some form or in the "seed" of past events.

- Know the most compelling aspirations people imagine for themselves and show them how to reach them.

Engage All Five Senses

How do you accentuate the neural responses people have when hearing stories?

- Paint detailed word pictures – bring all the senses into your description.

- Use metaphors, similes, graphic language to capture what something might feel like, taste like, sound like – add graphics, videos, media that are balanced and appropriate to the message.

Exercise

Brainstorm ideas below and then return to your first draft to layer in more evocative elements under these four areas.

Reason – How do you appeal to people's logic and intelligence?

Emotion – How do you know what emotions people are feeling (or want to feel) and how will you acknowledge, evoke, or mirror these emotions?

Imagination – How do you bring new thoughts into people's minds, thus allowing them to imagine new possibilities? Remember the power of metaphors.

Five Senses – How do you tap into the physical responses people can have when hearing a story? What details help people experience their senses?

Delivery & Impact – "Where are we going?"

Tips and Techniques for a Memorable Delivery

Style

- Keep the storytelling focused, simple, and clear – avoid "trying out" dramatic flourishes that may not be comfortable for you

- Tell the story as if you were talking to a single individual

- Tape the presentation to observe body language and movement

- Use visual aids judiciously and only use PowerPoint slides to amplify a point after the fact – lead with the message, not the slide – avoid having the presentation software dominate

- If PowerPoint is appropriate, use the Guy Kawasaki 10-20-30 Rule – no more than 10 slides, lasting no longer than 20 minutes, and have no text less than 30 point font

- Know how to use the voice, supported by good breath and use of the diaphragm for volume and strength – breathe **in** vs. using um, uh, or other verbal ticks – and use pauses for pacing

Delivery

- Know about the layout of the location you will be presenting, take control of any environmental aspects to avoid glitches like poor seating, poor acoustics, etc.

- Get out from behind the podium, remove barriers between you and the people in the room

- Connect with all parts of the audience through eye contact

- Slow down – typically nervousness or inexperience cause speakers to go too quickly

- Speak in an impromptu manner, avoid reading or sounding scripted

- Use gestures, and use the entire body to illustrate points or emphasize words and phrases appropriate to the venue (stage, meeting room, video clip, one on one, etc.) – natural movement that does not distract from the message is desirable, avoid planning a gesture that can come across canned

  - Recreate conversations or scenes to take people to important conversations, conveying the entire realm of sensations and emotions – this is what people are doing in their brains already so strengthen this experience

Go Deeper

Platform skills: getting skilled coaching for public presentations can ensure that you are prepared on all levels; verbal skills, use of voice and body, effective audio/visual support, how to handle the press, fielding questions, video do's and don'ts, etc.

Engaging Others

A Strategic Narrative has the power to bring a new reality into being. The act of sharing the Strategic Narrative strengthens the bonds among the people in the organization through the conversations about what they have heard. It's the sharing of the emotional responses that people have to the narrative that connects everyone at a personal level. This is a critical process for constructing cohesive social systems.

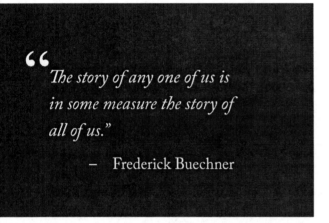

" *The story of any one of us is in some measure the story of all of us.*"

— Frederick Buechner

As stated earlier, engaging others "early and often" is critical for buy in when formulating a new strategy. This is a basic truism of good leadership. The more complex the problems facing the organization, the more helpful it can be to leverage the collective intelligence during the Environment Scan and decision making along the way.

In summary, engage people as much as possible in:

- data collection and sharing of opinions on what they see as the most important facts for understanding the current state

- investigating and sharing interpretations of what they view as events that have shaped the current state (positives, conflicts, losses, specific situations)

- formulating the metaphors to use and selecting the words that best reflect the priority values

- helping prepare versions of a Strategic Narrative that are appropriate for many different situations and audiences, e.g., short and long versions, visual aids to support the message, messages suitable for different media, outbound communications that impact branding and marketing, etc.

Examples of Strategic Narratives

Phil Condit, Past CEO of Boeing

Read the following text and compare it to the themes Phil Condit used in the other two samples of his speeches provided in the guide on pages 63-71. Seeing all three is instructive about the migration of a message over time. Because of Phil Condit's fine use of storytelling and narrative during his career and the availability of his speeches, we get a rare glimpse into the very skilled use, over time, of this methodology.

Rotary Club of Seattle, March 22, 2000

It took a while for me to get here. Jim invited me a year ago; I just finally found the way. It is always delightful to talk to Rotary. The serious, "reverent" approach that this group has (laughter) always makes me feel at home and welcome. So I will try to be equally serious and reverent.

There are a lot of things that I could talk about today… that I could talk about with a great deal of passion. I could talk about the strike that we've just had and its causes and how it got resolved. I could talk about transportation in the Seattle area and tell Inner what I think needs to be done. There's a lot we need to do, and it's something that is vitally important to this area. As Shan said, I could talk about China PNTR and how important that is and how important world trading system is. I could talk about arts and Seattle, and why all of you ought to make sure that your subscriptions to ACT are updated because I'm the president of ACT. I could talk about education with tremendous passion, and I could talk about Boy Scouts with equal passion.

But we don't have that long so I'm going to talk about the future of Boeing, a subject that I can really get passionate about… about transforming Boeing as we enter a different age.

About the time many people thought that aerospace was becoming a mature industry, and in fact, that change had begun to slow down, suddenly the Information Revolution came along and the dot-com world arrived. And now we are into change at an unbelievable pace.

So some really interesting questions are, "What does the aerospace industry look like in a dot-com world? What does Boeing look like in a dot-com world? Two words: dramatically different. Now!

Boeing is a very different company than it was just a few years ago, and I will tell you right now it will be a very different company a few years from now.

The thing I'm saying to every single group that I talk to is we are going to do three things.

1. We are going to run a healthy core business.

2. We are going to leverage our core strengths into new products and new services.

3. We are going to open new frontiers.

Let's see if I can characterize that…

First, we are going to run a healthy core business. If you look at our various products… the things that you see every day. The facts are they won't look very much different, but the way we design them and build them will be radically different. The Information Revolution is changing the way we do those tasks. And the changes are every bit as profound as the impact of the Industrial Revolution.

Let me give you just one example; i.e., our current Joint Strike Fighter concept demonstrator. We designed two demonstrator airplanes… one that's a conventional strike fighter airplane and one that is a short take-off, vertical landing airplane. We designed in multiple sites around the world; i.e., in Seattle, St. Louis, in England and a number of other places. The pieces were assembled in Palmdale, California, into two different airplanes by a workforce of just 58 people. That's dramatically different. That's the kind of thing that's going to happen to allow us to run a healthy core business.

Second, we're going to leverage our strengths into new products and services. There is unbelievable potential for us… potential to supply support services and aerospace solutions to our commercial and military customers around the world. Part of this is happening because the world is changing.

Airlines are focusing on their core businesses; i.e., their service business of marketing their products, getting reservations, taking people from one point to another. They are much less interested in maintaining or modifying airplanes and that provides us with great opportunity. Those are products that we know.

That exact same thing is happening in the military area. The U.S. government once employed thousands and thousands of people in depots to maintain and modify aircraft. But they figured their job was to provide the defense, and they are now turning to private industry to do that modification and maintenance work. It's happening fast. Today, 25% of the revenue of our Military Airplanes and Missile Group comes from services.

Finally, there are enormous possibilities to open new frontiers. Let me give you just three examples, and the list can get really long. One, air infrastructure. Two, mobile communications. Three, e-commerce. Each one of those offers tremendous opportunities for The Boeing Company and its employees to do some pretty exciting things. I'm going to talk just briefly about each one of them.

First, air infrastructure. There is a great need today for what is (like all industries we come up with great names for things) Communication Navigation Surveillance and Air Traffic Management System (CNS/ATM). So from now on, it's CNS/ATM.

Let me give you the statistics. It took 45 years to reach a world fleet of 13,000 jet airplanes. That number will double within the next 16 years. In the 12 years from 1970 to 1982, the number of passengers on airplanes around the world doubled to about 750 million. Sixteen years later it had doubled again to 1.5 billion… greater than the population of China. By the time Boeing turns 100, in the year 2016, it will double again to more than 3 billion passengers a year.

Now what that means is that airports, and the CNS/ATM system, must contend with significant fleet and passenger growth in the years ahead. And that brings opportunity. Today's CNS/ATM system was literally first built up from bonfires on hills to lighted beacons on hilltops to radio beacons to omni-directional ranges and distance measuring equipment. It is all about a point-to-point, connected kind of system. The technology today would allow us to do satellite-based systems, provide communication to airplanes, surveillance of airplanes, management of airplanes on a global basis, and dramatically improve the system. I can't think of a better company than Boeing to attack that problem.

That brings another potential reward. Given the kind of data base the last Space Shuttle mission gathered… terrain data for the entire world… and the global positioning satellite system, it will be possible for every airplane to know exactly where it is. We have the potential to remove the cause of over half of all aircraft fatalities worldwide, a controlled flight of an airplane into terrain. You know where you are, you know where the terrain is, and you don't ever have to hit it. It's a tremendous opportunity for us and for the system.

Second, mobile communications on a global scale. There is a great opportunity to keep people connected anywhere and everywhere in the world… in the air or on the ground. While the average person is not yet connected all the time, we are headed in that direction and in one heck of a hurry. We are global, and we are becoming more mobile every day. We're on the move.

And there's a lot of room in here to use the knowledge that The Boeing Company has.

Most of us are lugging our laptops along with us. Why?… because we want to be connected; we want data; we want it now. And we'd really like it no matter where we are. I believe, over the next couple of years, we will go from the classic complaint of every traveling laptop user, which is, "Were you able to get connected last night?" to the automatic assumption that we can and will be connected wherever we are.

Let me give you just a personal example. Last year, I spent the equivalent of 75 eight-hour days in the air. And that is not my time to and from airplanes or standing around waiting… that's 75 eight-hour days in the air. Now the fact that much of that time was in an airplane, which has the ability to be connected, has changed my life entirely.

All of that time was productive. I was sending and receiving e-mail, which I get a lot. I was making, and I have to tell you a bit sadly receiving telephone calls. I was checking the stock market. I was working on speeches. In fact, making this speech is a little bit difficult for me because I normally put the final touches on a speech in the air and print as we are landing. Well, I didn't get on to an airplane today so I've been scribbling up here madly. It has become an integral part of my tool kit.

It allows me to be mobile and connected and that allows me to be out meeting face-to-face with critical customers, suppliers, with employees. It is the way we are headed. We need to be in touch with our business, we need to be out talking with people. Being mobile and connected allows me on a regular basis to send e-mail directly to 160,000 of our employees from anywhere in the world with a single keystroke. A few years ago, you couldn't even think about that.

Now a lot of you are travelers… think about this one a little bit. Today in a commercial airplane you have a few choices. You can read a book, use your laptop until the battery runs down. You can watch a limited choice of movies. Not very far in the future, you will be able to operate just like you do in your living room. You will be able to watch the Mariners game live, watch a Final Four basketball game, be able to send and receive e-mail, you'll be able to shop on-line or work on a report. The airplane will begin to look like your home or your office and has dramatic impacts on productivity. It will change air travel.

Once again, nobody knows highly mobile platforms, whether commercial or military, or satellites or space-based communication better than Boeing does. This is an area that is extremely exciting for us.

The third one of those examples is e-commerce. Boeing like every other corporation has tremendous opportunities. We've established, for example, an online spares operation and it has been an unbelievable success. In the next 24 hours, we will sell more than $1 million over the Internet at Boeing.com, putting us in the top five of all commercial Web sites.

And just a few weeks ago, we launched a New Ventures' activity to leverage our position in the aerospace industry and our capabilities in the e-commerce space. I encourage you, in the classic terms, "Watch this space," because we are going to be doing some really interesting things!

So what does all this change mean to Boeing? I think it means we must make really critical, important choices. We can choose how we are going to leverage our tremendous core strengths and capabilities or we can choose to try and stay in the "good old days." Now as most of us know if we think about it critically, they weren't really so good.

What most of us want are the benefits of progress without change. That isn't going to happen. We do have choices. We can move ahead and embrace the future or be swept away by the tide of change. I believe that we can choose to adapt, to learn new things, to give back to our industry, to our company, to our communities by staying positive, by being open to change, by doing things that create a better life.

I believe we can learn from some really interesting people... people like Gutenberg or Galileo or Morse or Bell or Ford or the Wright Brothers or my favorite three Bill's – Bill Boeing, Bill Allen, and Bill Gates, who put all the pieces together.

Now let me wrap this up.

We are going to run a healthy core business. We are going to leverage our strengths into the new products and services. And we're going to open new frontiers. We have great opportunity. In the 1800's Darwin said, "It is not the strongest of the species that survives, nor the most intelligent; it is the one that is most adaptable to change." So, in 2000, I say, "Boeing is the most adaptable to change. We will survive and we will flourish!"

Additional Examples of Strategic Narratives

Jim Greenwood, President and CEO of the Biotechnology Industry Organization (BIO), a biotechnology trade association based in Washington, D.C.

Follow this link to hear a powerful Strategic Narrative delivered by Jim Greenwood. He focuses on the need to leverage the resources and change the focus of the biotechnology industry. It is a good example to view because of the effective delivery, use of voice, and authenticity which bring impact to the words.

www.youtube.com/watch?v=-r-LINNYiTw

Steve Jobs, Deceased CEO of Apple

Steve Jobs telling the blended "Who are we?" and "Where are we going?" narratives in 1997 when he returned to Apple.

www.youtube.com/watch?v=PEHNrqPkefI

Note: Fast forward to the 5 minute mark on the video

Use this link to listen to an example of a difficult decision Steve Jobs had to make in 1997 and how he charts the path to the future for the audience.

www.youtube.com/watch?v=WxOp5mBY9IY&

Getting Feedback

From Individuals

First, socialize the message. Start with supportive allies. Then share it with progressively more critical allies before "going live." Be clear on what feedback is desired from each person. Be sure to include people who can provide insight into how the stories would be received by your intended audience.

Second, when you deliver the Strategic Narrative be sure to allow time for people to respond. It's particularly important to understand what "stuck" from the content but also to hear how the story impacted people. Ask what stories, words, or metaphors seemed to be the most memorable and why.

Third, take the feedback and refine the message with each telling. Let people know how their input has contributed to the newest iteration.

From Groups/Teams

Many of the suggestions above would apply when gathering feedback from teams, groups, or the entire organization. Appropriate to the organization's size, an on-going methodology, whether it is aided by technology or not, is needed. This is an adaptive approach to taking what is being learned from execution on a strategy to adjust the strategy accordingly. The methods have to be selected dependent upon your particular situation and the balance between emergent and deliberate strategic approaches.

Mintzberg and Waters have captured this concept very well in the graphic on page 115. Where the stars appear an organization should pause in the execution of the strategy and listen carefully for how the Strategic Narrative is being interpretedly used, and where it needs adjustment. Ideally, the Strategic Narrative is kept alive through retelling, revisiting, and revising.

Go Deeper

Tracking Systems: have in place the internal systems to gather honest, regular, and specific feedback on each phase of the Strategic Narrative roll out and execution. Using dynamic platforms such as wikis, customer feedback/CRMs, and interactive meetings such as Town Halls will be important for tracking progress and buy-in to the messaging.

114

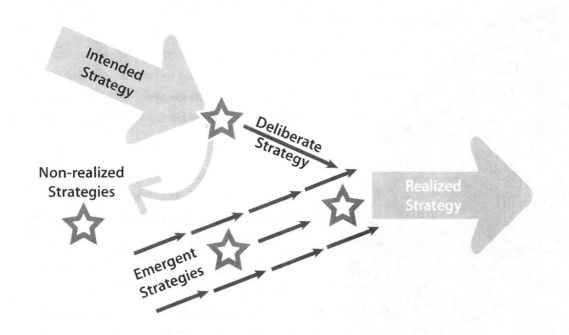

Mintzberg and Waters

115

Impact

Each organization has to decide on the best processes for tracking, measuring, and reporting on performance. Understanding the impact of the Strategic Narrative on the bottom line will ideally be reflected in the results due to greater engagement of the collective hearts and minds.

Specific ways to ensure that the Strategic Narrative and the stories that nest up into the larger narrative are working to produce the desired results are noted below. To go into detail on each of these is beyond the scope of this guide but references are provided in the bibliography.

Go Deeper

Dashboards & Score Cards: ensure that your planning process is transparent, visual, and can track both the deliberate as well as emergent elements of the execution. This will ensure that you are adapting as your organization learns and interacts with a constantly changing environment.

- Use stories aligned to the Strategic Narrative to sell to the customers

  - Use stories aligned to the Strategic Narrative to instruct or guide actions, particularly in areas where new behaviors are expected

  - Use stories aligned to the Strategic Narrative to build brand awareness and brand loyalty

  - Use stories that reflect achievements supportive of the Strategic Narrative such as positive outcomes and examples of unique approaches that produced impactful results

Learning fast and applying that learning can be a competitive advantage – individually and collectively.

The 3 Narratives – Summary

Types of Story	Who am I?	Who are we?	Where are we going?
Size – # of People	**One On One & Small Groups**	**Small and Large Groups**	**Large Group/ Meetings**
Typical Intent / Need	Connect Listening to learn about a new leader Builds trust Builds credibility Demonstrates authenticity & approachability	Remember Insight into action Reinforces change capabilities Builds team & self-esteem	Respond New concept needed and/or to evoke a specific emotional state Transfer Information Transform Action Sparks action Leads people into the future
Elements of the Story	Defining moments & key life experiences or influences Rich detail and personal values, implied or explicit, for teaching Personally meaningful	Examples of values in action – "do you remember when we did X and how that felt?" Real-life parables with a lesson or clear point(s)	Clarifies the current challenges Defines the steps to be taken Paints a picture of the opportunity once realized – what will success "look like, feel like"
What the Narrative Process Does	Explains why a leader does what they do Teaches others from their experiences Reveals a strength and/or vulnerability	Communicates a clear sense of identity Transmits & reinforces values Points out how what exists today can help the group face challenges tomorrow	Provides a strategic narrative or "new story" to replace the old one Engages and instructs others on how to win in the face of new challenges Shows the way to new values – guides further inquiry, sparks independent action

lead

language

speech-acts-create-new-worlds

journey

inside-out

mindfulness

Appendix

"*The place fate calls you to is the place where your deep gladness and the world's deep hunger meet.*"

– Frederick Buechner

A Confluence of Many Disciplines

A wide variety of disciplines, when put together, reveal why stories are so powerful. Once we understand these fundamental concepts about why narratives work, a leader can expand their use of stories even further. It's a challenge to briefly cover so many theories. I will try to do that and hopefully provoke further study.

This brief review will touch on bodies of knowledge within key disciplines which are the most relevant to the methods in the guide. The bibliography has two to three books from each of these disciplines should the reader want to do further readings.

1. Interpretive Management Theory

Beyond the human narrative imperative, storytelling is the way we create and recreate our realities and ourselves. This is consistent with **interpretive management theory**. The interpretive process encompasses written, verbal, and nonverbal forms of communication as well as pre-conditions that affect communication, such as assumptions, and values based meaning.

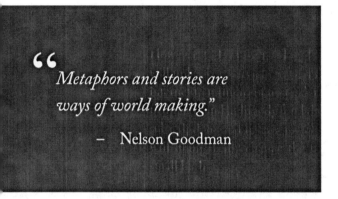

Metaphors and stories are ways of world making."

– Nelson Goodman

Knowing your audience begins with knowing what values and assumptions they currently use as guides for decisions and actions. This is the basis of their structure of interpretation. The leader will need a developed understanding of their priority values. A leader cannot bring a new reality into being without understanding the current reality they are building upon and where their values merge or diverge with the people they are leading.

The act of individual interpretation is not a stimulus response phenomena but a personally generated reality. Our internal reality is constructed from a field of meaning or a discreet set of values which we project out into our world. Using the metaphor of a movie, we create the movie of our lives as we experience it moment to moment vs. stepping into a movie which is external to us.

Richard Kearney wrote in, "*On Stories*," about how we build a shareable world when "haphazard happenings are transformed into story and thus made memorable over time, (it is then) that we become full agents of our history… this involves a transition from the flux of events into a meaningful social… community."

It's not just storytelling it's also the dynamic of story listening and interpretation of what is heard that is a dynamic, ever unfolding meaning making process. Leaders must understand the how, where, and when of the organization's process of interpretation to participate in it and shape it.

2. Social Constructionism

Storytelling is social. By listening for the stories about the history and looking for how the stories are represented in graphic or tangible form, a leader can tell a great deal about what matters. The stories capture the world people live in and provide the guidelines for how to build the social life of an organization.

We live in a world where our lives are shaped by the stories we create about that world. We do this individually and collectively.

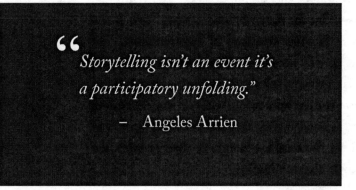

" *Storytelling isn't an event it's a participatory unfolding.*"

– Angeles Arrien

Social constructionism is a theory from sociology and psychology that believes cohesive groups construct knowledge for one another, creating shared stories, with shared meanings. When one is immersed within a culture of this sort, one is learning all the time about how to be a part of that culture on many levels. In this way, stories become an important artifact for culture building that guide the countless choices resulting in a shared social reality.

3. Cognitive Science

PowerPoint presentations typically do not help individuals in an organization to remember or engage in a course of action. Nor do the typical mission, vision, and strategy documents. They do not capture the whole in a way that guides, instructs and inspires discretionary action. Our cognitive function generates story lines as a way to organize for action. We need to thoroughly understand how stories are constructed to provide a coherent and compelling pathway for action.

Cognitive science and cognitive linguistics claims we are more effective when we understand the "whole" versus individual pieces. The "whole" is best captured by a story that conveys facts and emotional content. The "big picture" is typically conveyed by mission statements, or strategic plans. Often, these are in presentations with lists of facts vs. meaningful events or imagined events unfolding in time. Using narrative structure we can mirror the way our brains work, including facts and emotions within an easily remembered whole.

4. Linguistics

Stories begin with the most basic building blocks; words and metaphors. Listening for current vocabulary and metaphors and then bringing new vocabulary and metaphors into a culture can subtly change and re-direct the shared narrative. At times, a single metaphor, well thought out and well placed, can spark new imaginings and new possibilities.

Linguistics has provided us with an understanding of the power of metaphor, not simply as a characteristic of language but as a linguistic carrier of our conceptual frameworks. Words are worlds and metaphors capture these worlds which can mindlessly enslave us or set us free into states of our deliberate creation and choice.

5. Situated Cognition

Stories and storytelling must be authentic to build trust in the leader. Authenticity comes from walking the talk and also from the leader experiencing the full commitment to their words not just in their mind but throughout their entire body. Without this, audiences will not believe the leader's message. Authenticity of this type trumps style and polish every time.

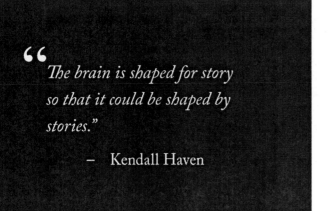

The brain is shaped for story so that it could be shaped by stories."

— Kendall Haven

Situated cognition puts forth the notion that knowing cannot be separate from doing, therefore all knowing is in the body (also referred to as embodied cognition). In other words, we cannot take the mind out of the body. This theory argues that all knowledge is situated in socially bound activity within cultural and physical contexts. So not only is our knowing in the body, it's also held within the shared social "body."

6. Neuroscience

What we are learning about the brain is influencing our understanding of why stories are a superior form of communicating. With the growing ability to map the brain's responses to stories we have learned what works when telling a story. Mapping our responses to stories show how the left and right brain, frontal and anterior lobes of the brain are all responding to stories as one brain vs. only portions of the left brain when presented lists such as we find in most PowerPoint presentations.

When the whole brain is responding to a story, the rates of retention go from remembering about 25% of what was heard to as high as 75%. When a story has emotional content, metaphors that trigger strong physical responses, and the story has organized the events into a temporal sequence we literally enter the story much like the Star Trek holo-deck experience where and imagined world is experienced as if it were real.

Other advancements in neuroscience are fast merging with linguistics, cognitive science and psychology to cross validate why stories are one of the most powerful methods for communicating complex ideas in a way that will be remembered.

The bibliography will provide some recommended reading if you choose to study some of these disciplines in depth.

Bibliography

Abram, David *The Spell of the Sensuous: Perception and Language in a More-Than-Human World*, Vintage Books, 1997

Anderson, Harlene *Conversation, Language and Possibilities*, BasicBooks, 1997

Baldwin, Christina *Storycatcher: Making Sense of Our Lives through the Power and Practice of Story*, New World Library, 2005

Booker, Christopher *The Seven Basic Plots: Why We Tell Stories*, Continuum International Publishing Group, 2004

Borowsky-Junge, Maxine *Creative Realities: the Search for Meanings*, University Press of America, 1998

Boyd, Brian *On the Origin of Stories: Evolution, Cognition, and Fiction*, Belknap Press of Harvard University Press, 2009

Carlzon, Jan *Moments of Truth*, Harper Perennial , 1987

Clarke, Boyd and **Crossland**, Ron *The Leader's Voice*, Select Books/The Tom Peters Press, 2002

Cron, Lisa *Wired for Story*, Ten Speed Press, 2012

Deal, Terrence E. and **Kennedy**, Allen A. *Corporate Cultures: the Rites and Rituals of Corporate Life*, Addison-Wesley Publishing Co., 1982

Denning, Stephen *The Leader's Guide to Storytelling: Mastering the Art and Discipline of Business Narrative*, John Wiley and Sons, Inc., 2011

Denning, Stephen *The Secret Language of Leadership: How Leaders Inspire Action Through Narrative*, John Wiley and Sons, 2007

Denning, Stephen *The Springboard: How Storytelling Ignites Action in Knowledge Era Organizations*, Butterworth-Heinemann, 2001

Drake, David B., **Brennan**, Dianne, **Goetz**, Kim *The Philosophy and Practice of Coaching: Insights and Issues for a New Era*, John Wiley and Sons, 2008

Duarte, Nancy *Resonate: Present Visual Stories that Transform Audiences*, John Wiley & Sons, Inc., 2010

Gardner, Howard *Leading Minds: An Anatomy of Leadership*, BasicBooks, 1995

Gottschall, Jonathan *The Storytelling Animal: How Stories Make Us Human*, Houghton Mifflin Harcourt, 2012

Haven, Kendall F. *Story Proof: The Science Behind the Startling Power of Story*, Libraries Unlimited, 2007

Heinrichs, Jay *Word Hero: A Fiendishly Clever Guide to Crafting the Lines that Get Laughs, Go Viral, and Live Forever*, Three Rivers Press, 2011

Herman, David *Basic Elements of Narrative*, Wiley-Blackwell, 2009

Kearney, Richard *On Stories: Thinking in Action*, Routledge Press, 2002

Kotter, John P. and **Heskett**, James L. *Corporate Culture and Performance*, The Free Press, 1992

Kotter, John P. *Leading Change*, Harvard Business School Press, 1996

Kovecses, Zoltan *Metaphor and Emotion: Language, Culture and Body in Human Feeling*, Cambridge University Press, 2000

Lakoff, George and **Johnson**, Mark *Metaphors We Live By*, University of Chicago Press, 1980

Loehr, Jim *The Power of Story*, Free Press, 2007

Marshall, Lisa *Speak the Truth and Point to Hope*, Kendall Hunt Publishing, 2004

McKee, Robert *Story: Substance, Structure, Style, and the Principles of Screenwriting*, Regan Books, 1997

Medina, John *Brain Rules*, Pear Press, 2008

Miller, Anne *Metaphorically Selling*, Chiron Associates, Inc., 2004

Parsons, Talcott *Social Structure and Personality*, The Free Press, 1970

Phillips, Andrea *A Creator's Guide to Transmedia Storytelling*, McGraw Hill Publishing, 2012

Pink, Daniel H. *A Whole New Mind: Why Right Brainers Will Rule*, Berkeley Publishing Group, 2005

Roam, Dan *The Back of the Napkin: Solving Problems and Selling Ideas with Pictures*, Penguin Books, 2010

Rock, David *Your Brain at Work*, Harper Business, 2009

Sachs, Jonah *Winning the Story Wars*, Harvard Business School Publishing, 2012

Scharmer, C. Otto *Theory U: Leading from the Future as it Emerges*, Society for Organizational Learning, 2007

Schein, Edgar H. *Organization Culture and Leadership*, Jossey-Bass, 4th Edition, 2010

Searle, John R. *Speech Acts: An Essay in the Philosophy of Language*, Cambridge University Press, 1969

Shaw, G., **Brown**, R., **Bromiley**, P. *Strategic Stories: How 3M is Rewriting Business Planning*, Harvard Business Review, May-June 1998

Shaw, Patricia *Changing Conversations in Organizations: A Complexity Approach to Change*, Routledge, 2002

Signorelli, Jim *Story Branding*, Greenleaf Book Group Press, 2012

Simmons, Annette *The Story Factor: Secrets of Influence from the Art of Storytelling*, Basic Books, Revised edition, 2006

Simmons, Annette *Whoever Tells the Best Story Wins*, American Management Association Press, 2007

Smith, Paul *Lead with a Story*, American Management Association Press, 2012

Snowden, D.J. *The Art and Science of Story*, Business Information Review, Issue 17 September 2000

Sussman, Linda *The Speech of the Grail: A Journey toward Speaking that Heals and Transforms*, Lindisfarne Books, 1995

Walsh, John *The Art of Storytelling*, Moody Publishing, 2003

Weick, Karl E. *Sensemaking in Organizations*, Sage Publications, 1995

White, Michael *Maps of Narrative Practice*, Norton Press, 2007

Williams, Robin *The Non-Designers Presentation Book*, Peachpit Press, 2010

Wortmann, Craig *What's Your Story: Using Stories to Ignite Performance and be More Successful*, Kaplan Publishing, 2006

An Invitation

This guide can stand alone and it's intended to provoke curiosity and further discovery. If you have purchased this book and are a practitioner in the field of Organizational Development, Change Management, Executive Coaching, or Executive Development please visit our website or send a request to the email provided below for a passkey to our Practitioner Community Wiki. We will speak with you about your interest and then you will be invited to establish a password allowing you to participate in our global community of practitioners.

www.ccs-consultinginc.com

Each of the three narratives have in-depth approaches which can enhance the guidance that practitioners provide a client, team, or training class when doing this work.

If you are a leader using this guide and would like guidance or questions answered please send us an email and we will get back to you as soon as possible.

Thank you for your interest!

Christine Cavanaugh-Simmons
President
CCS Consulting, Inc.
ccs@ccs-consultinginc.com

Gratitude

Definition: The heart's internal indicator on which the tally of gifts outweighs exchanges. International Encyclopedia of Ethics

To my long time business partner, Dave Ancel, who opened up the world of narrative theory that I will likely be exploring for the rest of my life. We have been partners in bringing that theory to real life application and the seeds of our earliest work are present in this guide.

Many thanks to Martha Lagare for her early reading and editing. Her ideas guided my re-writes and goal to get the "right" amount of detail and structure in the guide. To Wendy Appel, who shared all of her research on self publishing and the wisdom gained from her journey – she was and remains an inspiration to me.

And in the final stretch, Dr. Chené Swart has been a teacher and guide for my use of Michael White's amazing contributions from Narrative Therapy.

Of course to all of my dear friends within the community that I cherish, there are too many names to mention here but so many of you have encouraged me over the last two years. You likely don't know how much that helped and, corny as it sounds, you have been the wind beneath my wings.

Corey Ann Horton has and will hopefully always be my mainstay in life. I truly could not do what I do without her. She has supported me every step of the way.

Last and never least, my dear husband Steve who always makes me laugh and brings love into my life – every day.

About the Author

Christine Cavanaugh-Simmons is the President of CCS Consulting, Inc., a global coaching and consulting company based in California. Christine has been instrumental in developing a methodology in her coaching which uses narrative theory and effective approaches to storytelling for leaders. She uses this unique approach to assist her clients in developing strategic narratives, effective messages for driving change as well as individual leadership effectiveness.

Ms. Cavanaugh-Simmons has worked within fast growing small businesses and been a lifelong entrepreneur, starting and selling multiple small businesses over the span of 30 years.

Past leadership roles have been Regional Vice President for a Retail Chain, General Manager for a West Coast based consultancy, and Western Regional Vice President of an East Coast based national training consulting firm.

Ms. Cavanaugh-Simmons has worked for many years with technical, healthcare, and retail clients. Some of her clients include Oracle Corporation, Applied Materials, Kaiser Permanente, Salesforce.com, SAP, Haas Business School, Brown-Forman, Hewlett Foundation, Cephied, Intuitive Surgical, Shell Oil of Canada, and Symantec.

Christine graduated Magna Cum Laude from San Francisco State University with a degree in Psychiatric Social Work and subsequently worked as a therapeutic professional in Community Mental Health in San Francisco and at USF's Children's Psychiatric Unit.

CPSIA information can be obtained at www.ICGtesting.com
Printed in the USA
LVOW09s2325281013

358946LV00006B/856/P